Silk Hats
and No Breakfast

DP43
T7
1958

SILK HATS
AND
NO BREAKFAST

Notes on
a Spanish Journey

HONOR TRACY

Random House New York

67470

MAR 1961

THIRD PRINTING.

Published 1958 in the United States.

© *Copyright, 1956, 1957, by Honor Tracy.*

All rights reserved under International and Pan-American Copyright Conventions.

Library of Congress Catalog Card Number: 58-5262

Manufactured in the United States of America.

To Don Juan

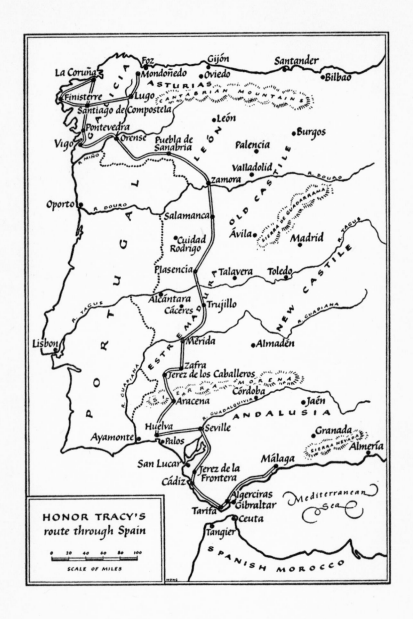

HONOR TRACY'S
route through Spain

0 20 40 60 80 100

SCALE OF MILES

Silk Hats
and No Breakfast

1

WHETHER GIBRALTAR should return to Spain or not is a question difficult to decide; but at least its way of life was Spanish enough for the hotel to have misinformed me about the departure of the ferry for Algeciras. It was only half an hour out, however, and joy at the prospect of entering Spain once more had brought me fussing down to the quay in plenty of time, so that the ferry was only just pushing off as the taxi arrived. The driver, again, was Spanish enough to leap from his place and address an impassioned appeal to the master: the ferry immediately pulled in, with a Spanish respect for the needs of the individual, or at any rate of the foreign individual; and then the vessel sturdily ploughed its way into the gold and silver haze of the morning towards the hills of the mainland, still green in this early June.

Very soon the little fighter planes that buzz angrily about the Rock were left behind: left behind too were order, efficiency, cleanliness, peace and fair play. In an ecstasy of ingratitude I sat up on a bridge marked for the use of crew only, watching the dear, grim shores grow nearer and nearer until at last the small figures of men could be seen moving about on their surface. What wouldn't some of these give to be making this journey in the opposite sense? How brilliant, how exotic, how much like a fairyland must seem to them that state of affairs from which we so thankfully hurry away! As far as I was concerned, they were welcome to all of it.

At Algeciras a Customs officer in shabby tunic and gleaming boots glanced at the whisky, coffee and cigarettes I had bought as a bribe to Gerald Brenan, and went on to more serious business. Travelling alone? And your husband, where is he? No husband! But there is still time. And so you have come here all by yourself. France is a long way off. My brother was once in Buenos Aires. Are you on holiday, perhaps? There was a hint of reserve in his manner which disappeared when I said that I was a writer, collecting the material for a book. A woman alone in Spain is an object of suspicion, as probably up to no good: it is slightly better if she is foreign, since foreigners notoriously have no idea of proper conduct; but if she is a writer she moves up into a special category of lunatics where ordinary rules no longer apply at all. The reassuring information was passed along the file patiently waiting its turn behind.

"I suppose you make a lot of money," the officer said and, sighing, chalked the bags.

The office of the Bank of Spain was shut and my currency declaration, with its printed warning of what might befall if every one of the formalities was not complied with, had to remain unstamped. Happy to be once more among unregulated people, I passed on towards the town. The man in the tourist bureau gave the necessary information about buses to Malaga and urged me to lose no time in catching one. Algeciras is a small town: there is nothing to see. Nothing. Well, yes, there is the Moorish aqueduct, but it is nothing. *Nada. Nada. Nada.* And the wine here is no good. I pointed to a yellow and crimson poster announcing a stupendous *fiesta* for the coming Sunday, but he shook his head with finality.

"*Nada,*" he said. It was a point of view both fresh and interesting in a promoter of tourism.

4

The pleasure of being in Spain at all left more particular considerations out, but it is true that not a great deal can be said for Algeciras. The seediness of Morocco appears to have crept over the Straits and set in here. An army of touts, beggars and pedlars of smuggled trash harry the stranger and, in the Arab way, take his refusal as a personal affront; and since he is unlikely to be there for more than a few hours, the attack has to be launched full-out from the moment of his appearance.

Yet the fifty minutes before the bus left for Malaga could be agreeably spent. Under the striped awnings of the cafés along the harbour-front people were laughing and talking with the reverberant Spanish buzz that makes English conversation sound like the hush in a cathedral. Competing, the guitarists strummed their Andalusian songs and surprising adaptations of American hit songs from many years ago. A fat man with a gold wrist-watch and, on his little finger, a sparkling diamond ring, his shirt open to reveal a mop of black fur, hesitated between two ties from a gay assortment. Should it be the scarlet satin with the bull's-head motif or the yellow silk with the black hoops? It would be terrible to make a mistake: his white, oily face was puckered with the worry of it. Two priests with blue chins and laughing eyes were enjoying a doubtless well-earned drink of Coca-Cola. The tiny boy at the table next to them preferred a glass or two of golden sherry, pressed on him by an adoring father.

I sat drinking cold beer and gazing contentedly about me. A boy with a shallow basket covered with a napkin approached my table. But I wasn't going to buy any of his lovely prawns: I knew I wasn't. Such things are very expensive and I needed all my money for books, theatres, taxis to places of historic importance and other things of the mind. Gravely the boy withdrew the napkin. The exquisite creatures lay there in rows, their whiskers delicately curled, their plump bodies a creamy pink, their boiled eyes fixed in an appalled blue stare. I shook my head.

"*Si, si,*" the boy said, gently, as one who had the welfare of others at heart.

"I don't like them, really."

He looked doubtful at this and, choosing one of the fattest, carefully peeled it and handed it to me.

"You will like that one," he said. "It was still in the sea this morning."

Well, it was only twenty pesetas for six. Just this once. In future I should be firm. They needn't suppose they'll have it all their way with an experienced traveller like me, I thought, handing the money over. I'm not one of their green tourists, I thought, adding another five pesetas for the boy's dazzling smile. Twenty-five pesetas: the best part of five shillings; painlessly extracted in the twinkling of an eye. This shall never happen again, I told myself.

Of course it would happen again.

Presently it was time to board the coach for Malaga. It was a shiny monster with an indefinable menace glaring out of its great headlights, but provided with comfortable leather seats, first class in front, second to the rear and all efficiently numbered and reserved. Before we could get in, there was another set of Customs to be gone through. I remembered that the last time I made this journey I had passed through the two *aduanas* in Algeciras, armed Customs officers had stopped the coach on the road and there had been a further inspection at Malaga itself. This was said to be due to the fact that smuggling from Gibraltar was one of the staple industries of the region; but the curious thing about it was that not one of the officials concerned ever made a real inspection, of my luggage or anyone else's. They were simply items on General Franco's payroll, carrying out phantom duties for all but phantom wages.

Round the coach passionate farewells were being said, as

always when the members of a Spanish family have to be separated by a few miles for a day or two. Inside it, passengers were carefully drawing the little blinds in order to exclude the sun. The driver put on his smoked glasses and with dignity assumed the peaked cap he would lay aside the instant we left the town. With a last outcry from the bereaved we were off.

Having secured a window seat, I pulled the curtain back and prepared to enjoy the view; but the pressure of silent misery from my neighbour grew steadily greater and after a mile or so I gave in. Brief glimpses through a crack were to be all: of the high eucalyptus trees waving their feathery arms above the white dusty road, coarse, fleshy cactus with frilly yellow blossom or rosy fruit, families of baby pigs, brown and glossy as water-rats, mean, bony mules and, now and again, under a broad straw hat a wonderful face, lined and brown, full of pride, humour and patience. My neighbour tried to make up for the disappointment to me with the half of a cold, oily omelet from his basket and a steady flow of conversation.

At one point the road narrowed suddenly, just as another coach came tearing up from the opposite direction. It was a case for one or other to slow down and pull into the side; but the question was, of course, which should do it, a question involving so many points as not to be seriously considered by either. Proudly our driver trod on the accelerator while his opponent did the same: the coaches thundered on towards each other like knights of old on the jousting field and passed with nothing more than a deafening crash and the loss to both sides of some paint. The driver glanced round with a grin of satisfaction and received the warm applause of us all for having maintained our honour.

At last the coach rolled into Malaga and drew up outside an impressive new bus station, with polished floors, ticket offices, cloakrooms, checkroom, a most up-to-date leather and chromium bar and everything appropriate to the New Spain; but at the same time, and as if it were impossible to see to everything at once, the crowd of hungry, ragged porters still was there, fighting for a chance to haul bulky suitcases through the baking streets for a peseta or two. I left my luggage and went to a hotel, listed as third class, but spotlessly clean, where the service has that peculiar Spanish quality of friendly nonchalance and the staff that rich assortment of personalities that bring back the traveller over and over again. But *"Nada, nada!"* shouted the receptionist as I came into the hall: the pain of having to refuse made him sound really annoyed. It was the eve of Corpus Christi and the place was flooded with French pilgrims; and there indeed the dear souls were, more incorrigibly bourgeois than ever in this Spanish setting, on the one hand shrilly exclaiming at the cheapness of everything, and on the other fiercely contesting each peseta from force of habit.

There was nothing for it but to set out again in search of a roof for the night. In the streets preparations were going forward for the great feast of the morrow. National and Party flags waved from public buildings, for this Government has requisitioned the Faith entirely. At one end of the Alameda was a curious erection, suggestive from a distance of a vast gold ball hovering over an egg-cup, which turned out to be a giant host and chalice of cardboard, placed on a temporary altar simply and pleasantly decorated with green branches, but picked out with a fringe of multi-coloured electric lights in the usual blend of charm and vulgarity. The way that the procession would take from the Cathedral to this altar was being strewn with rushes; nets, like those used for trapping little birds, were going up on each side of it and awnings placed here and there overhead, no doubt for the protection of clerical pates from the noonday sun. In a square off the main street another altar was being hastily run up to house the Virgin and Child. Men swaying precariously on the tops of ladders shouted to their mates knee-deep in pink and white carnations on the ground:

8

all worked with grim intentness in the dual purpose of suitably honouring the Body of Christ and holding their own against Granada.

A hotel soon was found halfway down the Larios, so that there would be a fine free view of the procession from the balcony in the morning. The porter hastened away to fetch my bags. Only one little chore remained before I could give myself up to the pleasures of contemplation. On the following afternoon Gerald Brenan and his wife would be expecting me at Churriana, a few miles out in the countryside, and since all would be upside down with the *fiesta* it seemed prudent to find out now when the bus left, and from where. The proprietor of the hotel was unable to help. But many small local buses left from the end of the Alameda near the port, where the trees threw a delicious shade, and thither I went to consult the policeman on point duty. But as I stepped off the pavement, he trilled sharply on his whistle. In this land of irremediable anarchy, of total administrative confusion, of lost files and dead letters and disregarded law, I had broken the single rule which always and everywhere has to be observed: I was attempting to cross the road at the wrong point. Abashed, I crept round in a wide detour and was rewarded with a courteous salute and a smile of forgiveness. The bus for Churriana left from just near by, first to the right, then to the left, then right again and there would be a little square. Another salute, another smile: *Nada, nada.*

In the little square the people disclaimed all knowledge of a Churriana bus. A tiny, dispirited vehicle did stand there, its roof piled with hens, wine-bottles and vegetables, its interior crammed with jovial countrymen, but it was going somewhere else. If it would not do instead, if in a queer foreign way I was bent on Churriana or nothing, I must return whence I had come to the trees of the Alameda. There was nothing to wonder at in this. It has happened before that a Spanish policeman was unaware of a bus that left several times a day about twenty yards from where, for years, he had stood on duty. I went back to the Alameda, slinking furtively through the trees lest the policeman should see me and feel wounded in his prestige. In the open-air café waiters were darting to and fro with trays of coffee, beer, cakes and ices: were they, perhaps, more observant than policemen? I asked one of them. Carefully he set down a rainbow ice before a dignified gentleman with a long silver beard and turned, entirely at my disposal.

"The bus for Churriana," he said, pointing decisively into the green shadows, "leaves from there."

Where?

"There, there," he said, patiently.

A passer-by stopped dead in his tracks and asked: "What does she want?"

"The bus for Churriana."

"It leaves from the new bus station."

"*Hombre!* It goes from over there."

An altercation broke out, in which many others joined. Voices were raised. A splinter movement held that there was no bus to Churriana at all, but only a small train. The great majority refused even to admit this. The gentleman with the rainbow ice was appealed to and, with all the weight of his beard, came down for the bus-station party. Discomfited, the waiter shrugged and turned away.

"Anyhow, she has missed it," he called over his shoulder.

The men in charge of the bus station were mildly vexed at the idea that a bus for Churriana could ever darken their doors. Their coaches went to Seville and Alicante and Granada, fine upstanding things that they were. You had better go, they said, to the Alameda and ask the policeman on duty there. Deep inside me there now began a stirring and twitching, not unlike the movement of water as it comes to the boil: it is a sensation familiar to travellers in this country, and one that, if not checked at once, can lead to horrible explosions.

It seemed best to make a clean break and a fresh start and to concentrate my powers on finding the small train. That it existed was sure, for I had been in it once: it was a dear, mad little toy with its own little station, and it toddled very gently and slowly along the coast for a while before tacking inland of a sudden and incontinently discharging its passengers miles from anywhere. I went out once more into what I was beginning to think of as "the pitiless sunlight" and in a short space of time after only half a dozen or so inquiries arrived at the station.

"But why don't you take the bus?" asked the man in the ticket office.

"Because nobody knows where it starts!" I screamed.

"Here! It starts here!"

Here?

"Just outside this station. Everyone knows that," he assured me. "But the last one has gone," he said mournfully. *Nada*, I was merely finding out for tomorrow; and at this he raised his head and gave me a long, astonished stare.

A fondness for Malaga is, perhaps, a special or acquired taste. There are interesting and beautiful things to be seen there, but nothing superb. The Cathedral itself is chiefly endearing for what it hasn't: namely, the second of the twin towers which for lack either of money or impulse never was built, so that the edifice stands today as a one-armed giant, affectionately known to the populace as La Manquita. The gardens are lovely with their brilliant lawns, tall smooth-leaved trees and flights of delicate blossom, tended and groomed in the careful Spanish way; and the small public library set up in the very heart of it shows a generous and unbureaucratic imagination. There is the quiet dignity of the precincts and the Bishop's palace and the charm of narrow twisting streets in the old town, with their gay flower-booths and vegetable markets, and the bright, vivid life of cheap eating-houses and taverns. But round the corner from the showplaces, a step from the flashy window displays in the Larios, is a terrible and killing poverty. Despair looks out of the people's eyes in these quarters of comfortless age and hopeless youth. The same is true of many parts of Spain, particularly in the south, so that at times the foreigner seems to be sailing comfortably in a private craft through oceans of misery; but in Malaga there is a certain tang in the air, a bitterness, as if its people did not share in that humble acquiescence which makes the Spanish poor as a whole appear either saintly or mad. Red Malaga it was called once, before General Franco taught it Christian duty with his machine-guns; and perhaps the spirit of rebellion is not entirely quenched.

Whatever the reason, I am always glad to come back to this astringent town; and I now set off on a little tour of renewal and recollection. From one of the main squares I turned into an ancient, rambling house which is the British Institute and where two years before a most original and entertaining character had been in charge. This was a young man from the North Country who had visited Spain on a holiday and, as often happens, immediately succumbed to her charms, remaining there with little but mother wit to depend on until in time he was given the job of organizing English studies in Malaga. This he did with much success, at the same time becoming an authority on the life and customs of the port, so that an afternoon in his company was as instructive as amusing. Unlike so many Hispanophiles, however, he did not go native, but remained sturdily English to the core, even to making regular trips to Gibraltar to fetch supplies of the mouse-trap cheese and milk chocolate on which he mainly subsisted. He introduced me to a friend of his, a pretty Spanish girl of eighteen or so, who was putting money aside every month for her funeral. It was to be *lujo*, or first class, with three priests and black plumes for the horses, and I can see now the look of serene anticipation on her little face as she described it. But when I inquired for him now, he was gone; and the cultured young woman who seemed to have taken his place could give me no information.

There would be no one, then, to translate into homely Lancashire the salvoes that crackled off between the tiny street-urchins who, with their dark curls and great innocent eyes, put one in mind of the cherubs of Murillo: and who from the age of four upwards exhorted, admonished and apostrophized each other in terms to be found in no respectable dictionary. This thought came, with a poignant sense of loss, as I watched a French lady caress the head of one of them, inquiring his name and age. The infant responded with a single classic and lapidary phrase known even to me. *"Qu'il est mignon!"* the lady cried delightedly to her companion. *"Il dit que je suis sa mère."*

Down in the port a Spanish destroyer was in, and the ship's company was assembling on deck for the evening salute to the colours. The small white figures carried out the drill with a smartness and a precision never to be seen in the sister service, while the onlookers on the quay chuckled appreciatively. Perhaps it was the idea of Spain possessing a navy, or indeed anything at all, that diverted them, or perhaps they found a subtle comedy in the notion of discipline itself; but there they were, rooted to the spot until the ceremony was over, when they slowly and reluctantly dispersed, smiling as people retrospectively smile when they leave a theatre. A small boy took possession of me, explaining that Spain had many ships like this, but bigger, that Spanish ships were the best in the world and Spanish sailors afraid of nothing, not even thunder: adding urgently, as I moved away, that he was fond of ice cream.

The hours were passing, as they do in Spain, like the minutes in England. The golden glare of the afternoon gave way to a soft primrose shot with red and the mountains up the coast were a dark blue. As ever in the poetic fading of the light

13

my thoughts turned to sherry; and rather than be stared at in one of the cafés of the town, I strolled along to one that stood on the shore some way off, past the beaches where fishermen, in the morning, are to be seen dragging their heavy nets in from the depths of the sea: only to find as often as not that the dead weight that nearly bursts their blood-vessels contains more jellyfish than sardine. In this bar, which was also an excellent fish restaurant, were old acquaintances among the army of famished cats who went writhing and twisting like snakes from one table to the next, in the hope of a head or a skeleton or even, who knows, a piece of skin. Now and again, a token of what the night held in store, a rocket hissed up into the sky and exploded with a bang that recalled London evenings during the blitz; and when at last I reached the town again the streets were full of families, mother, father, children and babies in arms, blithely setting out to find places where the fireworks could be seen to the best advantage.

I dined in a restaurant with windows wide open to the warm night, but screened from the world by a wrought-iron grille through which came the soft wheedlings of beggars and lottery-ticket vendors, and of a man with a basket of cut sweet jasmine to sell: his praises of which mounted steadily in fervour and intensity until all at once, as if maddened by our obduracy, he burst into the restaurant itself, brushing the waiters aside, laid a sprig of the fragrant shrub on every table and, his basket empty, stalked speechless away into the night. And at half past eleven, as the revelry was about to get under way, I retired to bed, assured by the din that went on hour after hour, the bangs of rockets and crackers, the ringing of bells and booming of gongs, the screams of delighted children and the roars of the citizenry that I was truly in Spain once more.

2

THIS GREAT PEOPLE requires little sleep or none, at any rate
during the hours of darkness. The last sounds of night revelry
mingled with the homely ones of early morning, so that never
a moment of peace could throw its shadow on the happy
mood. Bells summoned the army of ladies veiled in black to
early Mass. From the cauldrons perched on their charcoal fires
at the curb came the fierce hiss of frying doughnuts. A knife-
grinder pushed his trolley along under the flowery arches
with the dignity of a bishop, fluting the sweet notes of his
call on a penny whistle. At the bakery on the corner a small
boy ordered and ate his breakfast: eight inches of dense corn
bread, split down the middle, freely sprinkled with greenish
oil and salted.

Already the processional route was lined with military in
hats with coquettish little tassels and uniforms of which the
tunic and trousers were usually out of sorts with each other.
Some of these soldiers had rifles with fixed bayonets and others
were grouped together round small machine-guns. Their presence at one of the happiest occasions of the Christian year
made a curious impression; but nothing could have been more
good-humoured than their demeanour as they took up their
position hours ahead of time, with the calm indifference to
boredom so remarkable in this lively race.

The fact that preparations had started betimes did not mean that the program would follow smoothly on. With all their love of religious display, the Spanish seem quite unable to work out the details beforehand in such a way as to prevent hitches in it, often of a ludicrous kind. Once in a small town I saw a *fiesta* where Our Lady was carried forth in state from the church to the main square. Nothing that love and devotion could think of had been forgotten: there were the young girls waiting to scatter their rose petals at her feet: and there was the triumphal car drowned in a foam of creamy blossom with the Virgin, dressed up to the nines, smiling down from the top of it: and there were the little arches, exquisitely decorated, through which she must pass. Unhappily, no one had thought of anything so dull as measurements; and as the car passed under the first arch, the Virgin's crown tipped drunkenly over one eye. Hastily it was righted and crammed down over the head with the scant ceremony permissible in these emergencies; but the second arch sent it flying altogether. A feverish consultation took place, and some of the young men in the guard of honour ran ahead, ruthlessly throwing the lovely arches down one after the other. And the people cheered and noticed nothing and threw their petals with the delicate courtesy of Spaniards to fellow beings in the distress of failure.

In the Cathedral normal usage had been relegated to a minor place. A flock of small dignitaries hurried purposefully through the shadows of the great building, arguing with each other and chasing old men and women away from their favourite saints to make room for carpets and chairs. A priest in a side chapel said Mass in what, even for a Spaniard, must have been record time, absently picking his ear as he did so; while his server had so many little chores to attend to that ever and anon he would bound lightly off to see about them, throwing the responses over his shoulder as he went. Humbly, the people submitted to everything.

As time went on the bigwigs began to collect outside the main Cathedral door: *falangistas* in white tunics, civil authorities in morning dress, the Army, the Navy, aglitter with medals and orders—given for what, one scarcely liked to think—gay with gold and lilac sashes, with every now and again a portly figure in cyclamen robes pushing through the crowd as one of the Canons put in a brief appearance.

At eleven o'clock the bells pealed out and the splendid throng moved gravely into the Cathedral, to be met by one more magnificent still, the Bishop, the canons and priests, gorgeously arrayed, men from the Orders in black and white or brown and acolytes in their winged surplices carrying lighted candles. While the people pressed back against wall or pillar, some vaguely falling on their knees in a pardonable confusion of idea, the great ones paraded solemnly before the High Altar, where the Sagradisima Majestad awaited them. Between him and the lower kind now stood a wall of sheer importance and indeed, as always among the pomps and shows of great Catholic ceremonies, both he and they seemed a little out of place.

To the singing of the choir, the Bishop lifted the Host from its place and carried it outside to a wooden car, smothered in white roses and carnations and adorned with fat cherubs, each with a white satin bow round its neck, while six of the paunchiest bigwigs, with the baggiest eyes, held a baldaquin over his head and the faithful knelt and blessed themselves as he went by. There followed an anxious moment as the Host was made secure, a wild lurch as the bearers got under way and then the car set off on its journey, shaking, creaking and trembling, while the train formed up to the rear in order of precedence, brought up by soldiers wearing German-style helmets and doing a passable imitation of the goose-step.

I went back to the hotel, threading my way as best I could through the packed bodies in the streets, to where the kindly proprietor had chairs in readiness along the balconies of his front and was himself surveying the multitudes below with intense enjoyment. Hours seemed to pass before the procession made its appearance again, for it had been fed along the way by parties from youth organizations, trade unions and others not important enough to figure in the ceremony at the Cathedral, yet still essential to the myth of pious unity. Bored and sullen they mostly looked, sweltering in their uniforms under the ferocious glare of the sun, while ecstatic ladies with dyed hair showered rose-petals on them from the windows above. Further delays were caused by the fact, apparently overlooked in the scheme, that the traffic of the town could not entirely come to a standstill and the throng had to be halted again and again while a tormented policeman allowed a lorry or two or a string of mules to cross the route.

"How do you like it? What do you think of it?" beamed the proprietor as they all stopped for the fourth time, the officers fidgeting with their swords and shifting from one leg to the other like restive horses.

Wonderful.

"It's very good for the tourist trade, this sort of thing," he remarked.

But unhappily I must break away and catch my bus.

"Ay! What a pity. And your luggage? The porter is watching from the other side of the street."

Perhaps the soldiers would allow him to cross.

The owner smiled skeptically and plunged into the interior, where he could presently be heard bawling at one of the chambermaids. It sounded as if she had been caught with her hand in the till, but in fact he was saying that somehow or other the porter would have to be fished up from his place. The rough tone that Spaniards use to those they pay is oddly in contrast with their politeness to strangers of whatever sort. The maid flew out of the hotel like an agitated hen and was instantly swallowed up in the crowd. Minutes ticked doggedly by and it

18

began to look as if I should never get to Churriana that day. But just as hope was dying the porter tore in with the sweat dripping from his face and, seizing up my bags, proceeded to buffet and cleave his way through the mob, utterly oblivious of all but the matter in hand while I, reared in a gentler or weaker school, toiled along in the wake panting "Excuse me! Sorry! We beg your pardon!" to his innumerable victims. Once he reached open ground he broke into an easy canter and I implored him to stop, for the back of his neck was a dark crimson and the bus was hardly worth the death of a good man; but "*Nada!*" he cried without looking back and gaily sprinted on. At the station he saw me off with exquisite politeness, bowing low and wishing me happy journey as if he had all the time in the world; and only as the driver started the engine did he go scorching back to the *fiesta*, in dread of missing another moment.

After the broken night and the heat and noise in Malaga, the calm of the little village was more delightful than ever. The Brenans' house stands a little way off from its center, a good solid building with good solid walls screening it from the road, from which the only sounds that come are the hoof-beats of mules and the creak of their carts, or the voices of children at play; and once inside the beautiful, shady garden nothing can be heard at all but the whispering of the fountain or the measured operations of the gardener. In this household there reigns a peace that is most un-Spanish and only to be found as a rule in monasteries perched thousands of feet up on mountain crags. My host and hostess gave me their usual friendly welcome, but —and it was a blow—they were quite unimpressed by the coffee I had bought with such care and hauled about with me everywhere lest it should lose itself. When last I had visited them, only two years ago, coffee had been a treat in Spain and the smugglers' cafés where it was served had to be tracked patiently down one by one: now, such was the improvement in things

19

in that short time, it was a commonplace. I had thought to see their eyes light up, and had intended the gift as a very small compensation for the intensive picking of brains that was about to begin: their soothing assurances that "coffee was always useful" were not the same thing at all.

They proposed that we hurry off for a swim at Torremolinos before the sun should leave the water. The way led up the long, dusty road which is Churriana's principal street and passed, among other buildings of interest, a farmhouse that was visibly going to rack and ruin, with sagging walls and dejected roof. The owner of it wished to get the tenant out, but was prevented by one of the fussy new laws that constitute such a threat to Spanish freedom: he had determined, therefore, simply to allow the whole thing to fall in over the tenant's head. When nothing but a pile of stones remained, it was true, he would have lost a valuable property: but he would have made his point, and in our sordid times it is refreshing to come on such fire and feeling, and such tenacity of principle.

All along the hilly path to the shore we talked about Spain and when at last we reached Torremolinos we sank into chairs at a café and talked about it further. Gerald Brenan knows the country as well as any Englishman alive and he shares his knowledge with the ignorant in a splendidly open way. When two or three English people are gathered together in the Iberian Peninsula inevitably at some point the question of animals comes up, and it was startling to hear him say that Spaniards love them as we do. They might think it unseemly, obsessed as they are with their own human dignity, to fondle a beast, but their attitude was not the cruel or indifferent one that foreigners supposed. He gave then what seemed a curious illustration of the argument: that when domestic creatures are old or sick the owners cannot bear to put them down but will push donkeys and mules over cliffs and leave them, perhaps with broken backs or legs, to die alone; and will turn unwanted dogs and cats loose to fend for themselves among the hundreds and hundreds of strays already starving. This unwillingness to take their lives directly, he thought, came down from the Moors: his wife put it down to stupidity and want of imagination: I wondered if it might be simply the helplessness of uneducated people anywhere. But Gerald Brenan said that the reluctance to tamper with life went through all classes and gave as example doctors, who will refuse morphine to an agonizing patient if it is likely to bring death any the sooner: adding, wryly, that this attitude disappeared at once the moment passions were aroused, as in the Civil War, when people would be slaughtered to left and right.

He told a story, delightfully at his own expense. I had said how much I would like to find out what Spaniards felt, if anything, about the hideous inconveniences of their country; whether they were ever irked by the taps that didn't work, the chains that didn't pull, the lights that wouldn't go on, and the impossibility of ever getting anywhere without changing at Bobadilla, or whether they soared above these trifles. He confessed that he wasn't sure; but he said that some while back, sitting in the same café with an English friend, this man had pointed indignantly to the holes that pitted the road and asked why nobody mended them. Brenan had immediately, in the defensive-possessive manner of the foreign resident, asked why they should: they did not mind the holes in their roads since they knew they were there and had wit enough to avoid them. But shortly after that conversation, in one dark night at the end of a *fiesta* in Malaga three hundred people had fallen into a hole in the street, caused by repairs to a water-main and left of course without any warning lights, and sixty of these poor people were injured so badly as to be taken to a hospital; and even to one of Brenan's *afición* it seemed to be going a little far.

The sun meanwhile was slowly going down and when we got to the beach the only patch of sea that caught its rays was at the mouth of a sewer, and we had to fall back on the chilly waters further along. As Gamel and I attempted to undress decently in the shelter of a fishing-boat, a youth came up and sat on the edge of it, treating us to a stare such as, outside of the Orient, is to be experienced only in Spain. The face is vacant, the mouth hangs slightly open and the whole power of the creature is concentrated in the two eyes that drink in the spectacle before them, unconscious of everything else and dead to shame. Brenan observed our predicament but, man-like, did nothing whatever about it, merely explaining as, somewhat ruffled, we joined him at the water's edge that foreigners were thought to be so loosely behaved as not to qualify for respectful treatment: and that the proper thing to do in these cases was to ask if there were no *vergüenza* in the *pueblo*.

This sounded indeed like a formidable two-pronged attack, for *vergüenza*—modesty, decent shame—lies at the very root of social ethics and a pride in the *pueblo* and anxiety for its fair name is one of the deepest Spanish sentiments. When, however, at a later stage of my journey and in similar distress, I was to fire it off and wait complacently for the collapse that should follow, the offender shook his head and smilingly said there was none.

"None whatever?" I faltered incredulously.

"Absolutely none," he confirmed.

It was the only piece of information or advice—but one—that Brenan gave me which was to prove inexact.

As we waited for the evening bus that should carry us a part of the way home, we had time to observe the population of the resort. It seemed to be largely Britannic, but stratified with a layer of summer vacationers superimposed on those regular denizens, based financially on Gibraltar, who lurk in the gin-swamps of the region all the year round. A meeting-place appeared to have been set up between the world of Mr. Butlin and that of Mr. Somerset Maugham, where subtle differences, no doubt invisible to the native eye, created a truly Saxon barrier of reserve and suspicion. Torremolinos is a place to hurry away from, from several points of view; but it does serve a purpose in collecting together one type of expatriate and holding it in a kind of reservation. At this hour of the day it was out in force, the men looking like elderly Boy Scouts, the women horribly trousered, herding in the various cafés and bars with a flap-flap-flap of *Daily Mail* and *Daily Telegraph*.

The brief visit to this pleasantest of households went by all too quickly. The mornings were spent, with spread map, in consultation with Brenan about the route I should take. I meant to make my way up through Extremadura and Castile to Galicia, travelling in short hops by the small local buses and staying in the modest inns of villages, hoping to see not only country that was new, but something of Spanish life away from the familiar paths and the great cities. Again, my host was a fountain of knowledge and generous help: all the best things done and seen in the months that followed arose out of his suggestions, and they were such as I could never have made for myself. Only one small issue remains between us, in no way impairing the veneration I feel for this profound scholar and excellent man, but trembling on the air like the melancholy snap of a harp-string whenever I think of it: namely, the wild camels of Lebrija. When Brenan first spoke of them I was overjoyed, for there seemed a great confidence in writing yet another book on Spain at all and a description of a wild camel-hunt in a remote district ought, I reasoned, to provide half a dozen scintillating pages at least. Indeed, so fired was my imagination, I all but had them written before ever leaving his house. But as I went on my way, eagerly questioning all I met, those camels grew ever vaguer and mistier. The nearer I drew to their alleged habitat, the more did their phantom outlines dwindle until at last in Jerez de la Frontera, under the satiric eyes of the Vice-Consul, they vanished into air and left only this shocking thought behind: could Brenan, perhaps, have been pulling my leg?

In the afternoon there we walked into the countryside, up hills dusty with olive trees and freaked with the bizarre shapes of cactus, through fields of young corn that men were carefully weeding foot by foot, and along paths bright with many strange flowers. Of these my hosts knew all the names, in contrast to the incurious native who is apt to answer questions with "Oh, just a *fiorito del campo*," or "Oh, that. That's no good to eat," assuming that with this information all interest in the matter must end. A respectful visit was paid to the cemetery to view the last resting-place of Picasso's aunt; and here we came on a sexton in the old comic tradition who inquired repeatedly if Aunt Picasso were male or female and only after long rumination, soliloquy and rubbing of chin led us to a niche in a crumbling wall, the home of spiders and lizards and unnamed, he told us, because the family had made no arrangements.

After a couple of days I said good-bye to these good friends and set off again to Algeciras, where my journey was to begin. I had been instructed, entertained, fed, comforted and given excellent advice, including the name of a stomach powder to which I probably owe my life. Brenan came into Malaga with me: we had a last discussion in the café under the trees of the Alameda: then, having seen me into the coach and my bags on top of it, and not, as so easily happens, on some other quite unrelated vehicle, he waved a good-bye.

3

ON THE MORNING of the *fiesta* at Algeciras, which was to be *estupenda* according to the official posters and nothing at all according to the official spokesman, the town awoke to the steady fall of rain. The place wore the woebegone expression of Mediterranean towns in bad weather: the white walls and honey-coloured roofs, the orange trees with thick yellow fruit still hanging on their boughs, assumed in the grey mist an unreal, theatrical air: the sad horses, ribbed like a cockleshell, hung down their old heads and shut their eyes as if this new blow were really too much. Bowed figures with light summer jackets shawling their heads crept through the lakes that were quickly forming in every street. The sea and the sky were one wet, silvery blanket.

A nervousness could be felt among all the inhabitants. It is nothing, they said: it will pass, it will be all right. But their anxious faces proved they were none too sure. They had been looking forward to dancing and singing and drinking. In the afternoon there were six beautiful, wild, indomitable bulls (the posters said) to be killed by those inenarrably valiant swordsmen, Girón, Ordoñez and Pedrés. Sideshows there would be, booths where you tried your skill and discovered your future, where you drank your *copitas* and ate all manner of titbits, where comic or frightening spectacles were to be relished to the accompaniment of delightfully ear-splitting music. It was the big day of their summer: it was a long time to wait before it came round again; and life in between was hard and dull. Reproachfully, they looked at the weeping sky.

At noon a feeble little brass band came out and tentatively paraded the town. Behind them swayed and tottered the huge carnival figures of a Negro man and woman in long, bedraggled robes, grinning a fixed, white, stupid grin and followed by the small *cabezudos* and a tiny, two-legged bull whose fierce little rushes at the children provoked screams of terror and joy. But no sooner had they reached the open ground in front of the harbour than the rain came down with fresh insistence and they flew for shelter, bull and giants and *cabezudos* flattening themselves against the wall like everyone else.

A man sat in a grimy charcoal store the size of a large packing-case, staring dreamily at the sky, and I asked leave to shelter on the porch. With a splendid movement of his arm he made me free of the entire hovel, as a nobleman might of a palace, and returned to his contemplation.

Presently the rain slackened a little and the tinny notes of the band and the shouts of the citizenry were heard again. The resolute townspeople all flocked out and prepared to make the best of things. A street singer took up his position, a woman each side of him, one with a baby in her arms, while a boy distributed the printed words of the song to the audience. The man, a squat, straw-haired, pug-faced creature, burst nasally into an interminable romantic ballad, the women supporting him with their hard, birdlike voices. On and on they went with faces empty of all expression, a tone that never varied and a complete lack of self-consciousness, while the crowd listened avidly with the same utter, childlike absorption. Splats of rain fell on them all from time to time but, spellbound, they never stirred: and the curious part of it was that the ballad was so extravagantly foolish as almost to have no meaning at all.

Suddenly, at last, it seemed from one moment to another, the rain stopped. The sun came out, the clouds sailed away and the sky grew serene and blue. A burst of sound followed as voices, muted till then in apprehension, regained their normal pitch. In the twinkling of an eye the cafés were filled with laughing, shouting people wearing their best clothes. Tiny boys, close-trousered and wide-hatted in the Andaluz style, and their sisters in long, frilly gypsy skirts, their pigtails stately piled on their little heads and jewels sparkling and dancing in their ears, were hugged and kissed and pressed to strong drink. The goodness of God was freely remarked on, and the face of Algeciras was one great beaming smile.

As soon as the doors of the bull-ring opened people with tickets for the cheap sunny side flew in to get the places that would fall into shade as the afternoon wore on; and then sat tranquilly down to bake for an hour or so on the stone benches, their heads covered with paper like roasting fowl. Those with expensive seats appeared in a lordly fashion at the last moment and were still arguing and shoving and expostulating when the arena gates were flung back and the band of the Guardia Civil entered to a gay *pasodoble*. Nor could they settle then until they had spotted their friends and established contact with them one by one. "José!" a man would bellow above the uproar. "José!! JOSÉ!!!" At last José would look round and with a cry of rapture spring to his feet. Signals were frantically exchanged, greetings thundered back and forth until at last it was enough for both parties and, deeply content, they could direct their attention elsewhere. "Angelito!" came then in ringing tones. "Rafael!!" Marching round the arena, the band played merrily on while the fever of the public steadily mounted. Enormous ladies groaned their way upwards, exclaiming at the heat and followed by strings of children. Foreigners could be heard explaining, with importance, the art of the bull-ring to each other. The whirr of a movie camera came from a bunch of American tourists as a young woman tricked out in comb, mantilla, red carnation behind ear and trailing dress took her place, looking remarkably silly. A fat cavalry officer leaped up with a cry of rage as a little boy poured sherry over his spotless yellow breeches.

The police began shouting at the vendors of wine and water to collect up their bottles and go. To make things easy and comfortable, the customers threw the empties down to them: flying bottles came thick and fast from every quarter, some glancing off heads and shoulders, some crashing against the stone balustrades, others caught by the proprietors, who smiled and bowed their thanks. Applause broke out all round the ring as the band at last marched away, still tootling its jolly, incongruous tune.

Now came the march-past of the fighters. A picturesque scarecrow in black cloak and white ruff pranced in on a fiery but hideous nag, at which the audience spontaneously whistled and hooted with the pleasant idea of making it bolt. There followed the lesser *toreros*, burly men with a perpetual scowl for their dead ambition, their middle-aged contours unmercifully emphasized by skin-tight breeches. Fat picadors came next, jolting stiffly up and down on their blindfold, emaciated mounts, wicked lances under their arms. Then there gravely paced the three stars, their shoulders hunched and their faces stern, wearing their splendid capes like a sling, the little bun of hair at the back of their heads giving them, in their male pride, an air of perverse femininity. Last came the plumed horses whose task it would be to drag away each mound of bloodied meat that, twenty minutes before, had been all fire and rage. Solemnly the cortege paid its respects to the President: those no longer needed left the ring: the rest took their stations: there was a flourish of trumpets, followed by a pause in which the heart thumped painfully in the chest and the palms grew wet.

Now and again there are *corridas* from which one goes away

treading on air. The grace and beauty and daring of the man, the noble defiance of his enemy, raise the encounter from a mere spectacle to a work of art, absolute, complete in itself. On these rare occasions there comes a sense of grandeur that overwhelms pity, fear and disgust and leaves only awe at the so magnificent, so needless, display of human courage. For one of these there will be at least ten at which one is ashamed to assist, affairs of humbug and attitude, a cautious butchery masked by bravado. At such times one is inclined to wonder if the whole institution is not merely another aspect of the Spaniards' endless preoccupation with their virility, as empty and tedious as the eternal prating of sexual competence and triumph. It soon became all too clear into which category this afternoon would fall. There was not a single clean kill: the picadors were inept and savage by even their own debased standards, arousing storm after storm of protesting whistles from the crowd: the matadors went slowly to pieces, as even the finest do when the mysterious fates of the ring are against them, posturing and strutting the more as their hearts failed. The people, as ever, were merciless. A roar of derision went up as Girón, after theatrically kissing the blade of his sword, made a thrust that went wide of the mark. Scathing advice was bawled at the unfortunate men from all parts of the amphitheatre. A bull who gave one of them a nasty bang with his horn, splitting the breeches from thigh to knee, was cheered to the echo. In no other circumstances are Spaniards quite so Spanish.

Not today the sea of waving handkerchiefs, the hats and flowers in the ring, the men carried shoulder-high and the roar after roar of admiration and delight. When the last unhappy animal had at last been done to death, the gaudy finery was hastily packed into the ancient, bulging leather coffers and piled on top of the battered Rolls-Royce, and the valiant swordsmen with their hangers-on drove quietly and unobtrusively away.

The great moment of the great day had come and gone and

proved to be as dismal as a box of wet fireworks. The wretchedness of it hung over the dispersing multitude like the damp of the morning. So much hard-earned money wasted! For the matadors take their thousands whatever account of themselves they give in the ring, and the ferocity of the cheated crowd can be understood. Off they now streamed to the fair encamped about the arena to forget their disappointment bravely on merry-go-round or car-rink, in tavern and dance-hall. All night long they sang, shouted, clacked their castanets and wailed their ululatory *flamenco* until the stars turned pale in the sky and the first workaday stirring began in the harbour. Then, patient and inexhaustible, they took up their daily lives. In twelve months' time, who knew, if God were willing, they might have better luck.

4

CADIZ is a city of magic, like Cracow or Dublin, to set the mind
on fire at a turn of a corner. Beauties spring into view unexpectedly, making a casual walk through the narrow streets into
a feast of surprises and enchantments: a lilac façade on the sea-
front burning rosily in the afternoon sun: a church at dusk,
the doors wide open to display tall candles flickering about
the heavy gold intricacies of the High Altar: the bent figures
of old women creeping into a vigil for the dead, their hands
full of marguerites: a glimpse through an ancient doorway into
a patio brilliant with geraniums and morning-glory. The eye
is continually fed, the imagination stirred, by a train of spectacles as charming as if they had been contrived.

The pleasures of the visit were much increased by the hotel
into which, by a happy accident, I had wandered. Experience
rather than comfort being the aim of my journey, I had decided
on reaching a new town to surrender to the first tout that ac-
costed me and follow whither he led. Here I had fallen in with
one whose greed outran his discretion, for when he set down
my bags in the hall of the fourth-rate kip whose resplendent
name adorned his hat, it turned out that the place was full up
and had been for days. Every single day in Spain I resolved
anew to be placid and controlled, and every single day the dear
thing was too much for me again: and now with un-Spanish

rudeness I flounced out of the building and into the first hotel that offered. It chanced to be one full of drama and colour and life, the enjoyment of which was assisted by a most peculiar construction. From ground to roof in the center a great well rose, on which the bedrooms gave, each with its little railing, as on to a patio. There was no outside ventilation at all, the windows being simply thrown wide to such air as the interior possessed; and a shutter screened the inmate from the public eye while allowing him a perfect view of all that happened in the lounge below. Now and again, indeed, a guest would neglect to sling his shutter at the proper angle, thus affording to those on the same floor some interesting little scene of private life; and every word that was uttered, each homely sound, was plainly audible except when, as often happened, the French Lady Travelling Alone was strumming wildly on the piano in the salon. The lavatory, too, was of more than usual technical interest, for when the plug was pulled out there was a hissing noise and a stretch of floor in the far corner was slowly inundated, while the contents of the bowl remained calm and undisturbed.

Such matters, however, were specialized in their appeal. The true charm of the place lay in the rich types of humanity that passed through and the flow of incident between them. There was a tycoon with a great belly and a booming voice who terrorized the establishment with orders and complaints until he found that one of the porters came from the same obscure and remote *pueblo* as himself, after which he was as pleased and gentle as a baby. And the hotel wolf, scented and side-whiskered, who looked impudently at all the girls until the arrival of the middle-aged pair, the tiny, scared husband and the huge, angry wife, creaking in her black silk, with a face like a bulldog; and in this unlikely quarter the poor wolf lost his heart at once, circling enviously about the alarming figure as it grimly read the paper in the hall and heaving sighs that could be heard on the first floor. An American woman had the place upside down, crying robbery and murder, for a souvenir of Toledo which later proved to be, where she had put it, in her purse. Some animated scene was always in progress on this central stage, beautifully lit and with perfect acoustics, that one could follow reclining in comfort on the bed. And at dinnertime we all would assemble, each knowing so much about the rest, and eat our four courses with perfect dignity and composure under the blazing chandeliers.

At six o'clock I used to get up and go to a workman's café for breakfast. For about eightpence there was delicious, strong coffee, fresh bread and butter and enlivening conversation: in the hotel there would have been an assortment of stale, sugary cakes and a jug of cool, grey liquid tasting of nothing. There was also the pleasant early sun and the calm morning face of the city as dockers and fishermen went about their business. On the quays grubby little trawlers with one funnel and names like *The Star of Cadiz* or *The Flowers of the Ocean* were preparing to set out for the day's work. And in the late afternoon they would all come in and two thousand tons or so of fish would be laid out in the long, icy sheds with the greatest neatness and order, the crimson *langostino*, the *salve* like a thin silver blade, the purple rubbery octopus, enormous skates hideously grinning and *cigalas* with their delicate coral-tinted shell; and a little army of middlemen, brusque and impatient, with smooth white faces and large tummies would appear to take the catch from the thin, brown, smiling fishers and send it away to Madrid.

In such a place one could never tire of wandering about and waiting to see what would turn up next. It was here, in the Alameda Marqués de Comillas, that I came on a wonderful tree, a glorious being that surpassed in its extravagance the wildest fancies of Blake. Huge twin trunks rose from a tangle of bare roots with the graceful bends and twists of a dancer to flow into a profusion of boughs, each thicker at the base than a tree and rising and falling in loops to a spread of seventy feet or more, supporting in festoons the lesser boughs with their plump, lemon-shaped leaves which spread below them a green, mysterious gloom. It was a tree that might figure in some madman's dream and the privileged citizens of Cadiz strolling up and down never gave it a glance. Three old men sat on a bench in the evening sun near by, watching me with amusement, and I begged them to tell me its name. They said that as far as they knew it was a wild fig and chuckled a little to think that anyone should care.

But it was in the Alameda, too, that I first met the baby beggars of Cadiz. The sad little tribe, abominable and innocent at once, lurked in the gardens all day long, waiting for strangers whom they would harry with inflexible resolve and extraordinary impudence. They were so young that some of them could barely lisp out the word "peseta," and so sharp as already to know the foreigner from the native, on whom they never wasted their time. The moment they saw me they rushed up, noisily drawing attention to their scabby heads or sore eyes and holding out their tiny paws with an air of utter misery. Their assessment of my intelligence was of the lowest. One tot assured me there was a "dirty thing" on my back and, picking a weed off it, triumphantly demanded to be paid for the service; but the roots showed it was newly plucked from the earth and its presence on my clothing could only have been the work of her hands. A small boy begged passionately for money to buy bread: I pointed in silence to the loaf under his arm, and he said that he was minding this for a friend and couldn't expect a crumb of it for himself. At each piece of effrontery on the part of one, the rest set up a wild, appreciative cackle of laughter. For the sake of peace I gave a five-peseta note to the biggest, telling her it was for them all, at which she streaked away like a scalded cat with the others in full cry behind.

It occurred to me, watching these abandoned little souls, that it was now the time to make the acquaintance of the other Spain. Ever since I had arrived, I had been conscious that there were two: one that offered itself to the eyes and ears and seemed to be precisely as it always was, and another, new, bustling and high-minded, which lived on paper. To believe the official publications it was fast becoming a kind of welfare state, although, of course, with none of the secular materialism that existed in other, less favoured lands. I read the reports of rehousing, communal centers, cheap holidays, insurances and similar ingredients of social contentment; but I saw the country around me wear the same bitter, dejected face that I had known for twenty years.

And so I went to the Delegación Provincial de los Sindicales and asked for their help. I was passed from hand to hand, led up and down stone stairways and along echoing corridors until at last I reached an office where, among piles of documents, sat two female clerks. On the wall hung a crucifix, with a portrait of Franco to the left of it and one of José Antonio, the martyr and bully, to the right: the trinity of the Movement. After listening suspiciously to what I had to say, one of the clerks told me it was a matter for the Delegate himself; and he was in conference and would so remain for she could not say how long. She was a fat, blowsy woman of thirty-five or so, with dyed hair that was black at the roots, heavily made up and with grubby hands; and there was someone almost exactly like her in every Falangist office I ever saw.

Would I, she said, be kind enough to go away now and telephone tomorrow, asking for Rosita. And who was Rosita? She laid a grey hand on her breast. Very well. Early next morning I telephoned and was told that Rosita was in conference. No one could say for how long. I walked round to the Delegación and made my way to her sanctum, evading the half-hearted interceptions of numerous employees standing about the passages in attitudes of chronic under-employment. Rosita was enjoying a conversation with her fellow worker and she looked up frostily as I asked if the Delegate were free, and if not when he would be; for I would be glad to come whenever it suited him and be deeply and properly grateful for a few minutes of his time.

"The best thing will be," Rosita said, after thinking it over, "if you go away now and telephone in the morning."

There seemed no reason why this little pattern should ever be interrupted and I therefore went to see the British Consul. He was very willing to help, like most of his colleagues in Spain, and spoke with enthusiasm of what the Falange were doing, particularly of the Home of Culture and Rest for workers; and he at once gave me a personal introduction to the elusive Delegate.

Rosita looked really vexed when I reappeared and the words "*tiene visita*" immediately shaped themselves on her lips; but at the sight of the Consul's card she became suddenly wreathed in smiles. She tripped away into the Delegate's room and came back to say that a motor car and escort would be at my disposal that same afternoon. Lest she had not made herself clear she grasped an imaginary steering-wheel and remarked: "Brm! brm! brm! honk! honk!" She went so far as to wave as I left the office. Returning at three o'clock, I slid into the Delegate's presence as if buttered. He was a pleasant, coarse-grained young man with the rough, offhand style affected by Fascist and Communist officials everywhere. The office was large and handsomely furnished, with cigars on the table and on the wall the Falangist trinity again, Franco and José Antonio flanking the central figure as it might have been the two thieves. My escort, a very small man with a very big manner, was introduced and the pair of us set off together by car for a tour of the *viviendas*.

These are the working-class housing estates that are going

up at a great pace in many parts of the country. They consisted of square, severe buildings laid out in rows like a barracks and were divided into flats of varying sizes and rents. My escort knocked in a peremptory way on the door of one of them and we were at once admitted by a stout lady, most anxious to please, who showed us everything in the place down to the shower and the lavatory. It probably was no worse than many council houses in England and the rent was only a hundred and twenty-five pesetas a month; but the tenant did not seem to belong to the working class and, in fact, my escort said later that her husband owned a business. Afterwards we went on to the *vivienda* inhabited by my companion himself, which was larger and grander, with hot and cold water, bath, shower and *bidet*. It was furnished in perfect petit-bourgeois style with a bowl of artificial pink roses here, a tasteful reproduction there, cabinets of dainty china, antimacassars and of course a profusion of religious pictures and statues. A wife was produced for inspection, plump, bejewelled and painted, and a daughter of eight months, at which my escort became briefly human. He did not suggest that we enter any other apartments, and I wondered how many more of them, put up for the workers with such a fanfare, were in fact housing the officials of the Party and their friends.

The Home of Culture and Rest, again, was not more squalid than many English holiday camps and far less noisy. The rooms had three or four beds in each, or bunks one on top of the other, and there was a library, stocked chiefly, as far as I could judge at a glance, with religious and political tracts. General Franco stared impassively from the walls of the main assembly rooms. In the kitchen, where they were frying great steaks and piles of onions, the cooks looked up as my escort swaggered in and smiled brightly and dutifully. We saw the swimming pool, used by men and women at different times of the day, and the solarium for men, the solarium for women, and the entirely seg-regated home for young girls. Everything was clean, imper-sonal, comfortless.

In appearance and atmosphere the place was a faithful copy of similar establishments in the Communist lands; the inmates too had precisely that air, the staff nervous and deferential with the visitor from headquarters, commanding under their genial-ity with the guests who, once more, did not seem to be work-ing-class at all. My escort told me that they paid only ten pe-setas a day and could stay for a period of up to ten days. I asked where the balance of costs came from, and he said it was paid by the Delegación Provincial. This meant from the syndi-calist funds, and that, of course, meant from the members' con-tributions: which looked rather as if the real workers were helping to subsidize, through their forced payments, the recrea-tions of Party men, bureaucrats, police informers and other such props of the régime. A list of every soul in that place, with his occupation, would have been interesting; and interesting too was the fact that the Falange, when at last it turned its mind to constructive matters, could do no more than borrow the ideas of its enemy, even down to the very familiar-sounding title.

In the motor car on the way back, the bossy little man shed his importance and became jovial and entertaining as he de-scribed for me, bull by bull, the magnificent *corrida* they had there for Corpus Christi. That, with his baby daughter, was what really interested him, as it would be for any normal Span-iard. But he had certainly done his duty by me, asking only in return that I should be sure and tell the people abroad what the Falange was doing: he clearly believed it was something very splendid indeed.

Later in the evening I lost my way and wandered into the quarter where the people really do live, with the crumbling walls and the missing windows, the screaming children and starveling dogs, the lines of damp, dirty clothing and everywhere the smell of excrement. I sat for a while in a café where terrible figures that Goya might have painted visited the tables one by one: the epileptic, twitching and stuttering, with his tattered album of postcards, the crone bent nearly double with her lottery tickets, the dwarf photographer with the enormous head and the beautiful, wretched eyes, a procession of grotesques timidly yet insistently offering wares that nobody wanted until at last with a few sharp words a waiter would drive them away. And then, meditatively, I returned to the hotel and penned a line of thanks to the Delegación.

5

THE LITTLE TOWN of Arcos de la Frontera perches on the top
of a hill from which the sides fall away in steep cliffs, giving
it from a distance the air of a ship moored in the rolling plains
of the Guadalete. The bus from Jerez draws up at the foot and
the visitor climbs up a narrow cobbled street with whitewashed
houses on either side to the rich, immensely ornate Church of
Santa Maria, standing on the highest point of all: an edifice
which, as so often happens in rural Spain, is out of proportion
to the humble dwellings clustered around and below it and
gives the *pueblo* a top-heavy air. Inside and out it is a monument
to vanished splendour, with its huge, profusely decorated
doors, finely carved choir-stalls, heavy gold ornamentation of
chapels and lovely gothic roof. Blue tiles stand out like flowers
on the weathered grey stone of the bell-tower, while the body
of it is of the beautiful honey colour characteristic of the region.

Oddly let into the east side are curtained windows, all cosy
and domestic: pots of rosy geraniums peep through twisted
iron grilles; and incongruous on a balcony between the figures
of Peter and Paul this Sunday morning stood a youth in shirt-
sleeves smoking a cigar and surveying the scene far below him
with an air of proprietorship. The hour of the principal
Mass was not far off and a crowd of girls in light dresses,
their heads, arms and legs all modestly covered, paced briskly

up and down, meanwhile wagging their scissor-sharp tongues at emergency speed lest the summoning bell should ring before they had fully accounted for all their neighbours. Near by a tiny urchin sprawled on a mound of green pumpkins and, chewing a purple onion, watched them at it with the air of a man of sense and discretion.

There was all the time in the world, for the bus which had left Jerez at eight in the morning would not return before six in the afternoon; and I wandered down the main street once more to visit the other church, standing a little way off from the *pueblo*. The municipal garbage man was going his rounds, a fine figure of a man, five foot tall if an inch and penetrated to the marrow with his own importance. Leading a mule and cart, he would stroll for a few yards in a leisurely manner and then halt, blowing shrilly on a whistle, at which the housewives came running out with pails of garbage in their hands and tipped them in. He never spoke to the women or even glanced their way, but merely strolled and whistled, strolled and whistled, looking gravely ahead of him meanwhile: whether he was obsessed by the dignity of his function or trying to rise above it, I could not determine.

San Pedro too was old and mellow and a little big for the *pueblo*'s boots. On the bell-tower storks were standing deep in thought over their blowsy nests or flapping about in short, ungainly flights when they felt the need of change. The fresh-ness of the blue-tiled interior was agreeable after the blinding sun outside but there was little to see of interest, except for two delightful carvings in oak at the west end. Elsewhere were frightful plaster saints in robes of clean, starched linen, round which some nuns were clucking and mumbling like mothers preparing their daughters for a ball.

From a hill further on there were splendid views, one of the *pueblo* clinging to its peak and crowned by Santa Maria, one of the mile upon mile of silvery olive with red-tasselled

41

Indian corn standing in between the trees. A tinkle of bells, gay and melancholy at once, came from a field near by where a peasant was threshing wheat: there was to be no Sunday *paseo* for him. He stood in the middle of a flat space of earth with the grain spread over it in dusty yellow heaps and drove six fine horses, each pair attached to a long rope in his hand, round and round him like the ring-master in a circus. From the horses' necks dangled the little iron bells that gave out so plaintive and charming a music, and this was accompanied by the peasant himself who, unwearying, sang the same brief snatch of *flamenco* over and over again as if its beauty struck him ever afresh. Soon we were joined by the master who had ridden up to see how the work was going and who, in the friendliest way, asked a number of searching questions about my family and informed me completely as to his. And all through the countryside as I walked on the sound of bells came to my ears and in small clearings I would see other good horses faithfully circling and circling at the end of their ropes as they beat out the grain.

After a couple of hours, exhausted, I found a resting-place by the river below a weir with smooth, grey boulders to sit on, where I could dangle my feet in the rushing waters. The air was full of the scent of thyme, the earth gay with clumps of pink oleander which had crowded vigorously into every dip and gully with the least suspicion of dampness in it. There was no one in sight but half a dozen mules standing knee-deep in the water and meditatively switching their tails from side to side. Stranger still, there was not a sound to be heard except for the whispering of the river: it was, I think, my first moment of peace in Spain. Across the water rose up a sheer cliff of several hundred feet, ridged and crumbled like old cake, with scores of rust-coloured hawks wheeling and hovering over it and topped by Santa Maria again, more imposing than ever in the grandeur of the setting. Terrible work it must have been to drag up the materials for that great pile. The Greeks in their piety excused from further labour the oxen who once had taken part in such, and we must hope the wretches here at least have been suitably rewarded in heaven.

"*Señorita! Señorita!*" came in the tones of a startled corn-crake: the raised voice of a Spanish girl, that cleaves the skull and sets the teeth on edge. Two little maidens had espied me from far off and came hurrying up, in their engaging way, to put an end to my unnatural solitude. "*Solita!*" they shrieked compassionately, as one might exclaim: "But you have two heads!"

I dragged myself up and over the bridge and began once more the ascent of the long, baking hill. A bank of clay rose to one side of it and in this were a number of caves, barely large enough for a man to stand upright with any comfort but in which nevertheless families were living. Strewn about on the earth inside were the filthy sacks they slept on and the rusty pots they used for cooking; and yet each of these caves was neatly numbered, like villas in a suburban terrace, giving them a touching little air of self-respect.

It was time for luncheon by now and the single, dispiriting *fonda* was the only place to go. Here they provided a tomato, onion and cucumber salad, doused in pungent oil, followed by a wan soup with worms of vermicelli swimming to and fro in it; and this was followed by an interval. Then came tomato, onion and cucumber again, now fried in that same oil, and a solitary fried egg. At this point a bank of garlic drifted in from the kitchen like a sudden attack of poison gas, and the offer of fried veal cutlets was declined. The meal closed with a green banana.

I was waited on by a friendly, garrulous boy who found it hard to believe that I wanted half a bottle of red wine all to myself. Spaniards are frugal, austere people even in the relaxed south, and the drinking of a half pint of wine by a female strikes them as not far removed from an orgy; but for the kind of meal one undergoes in wayside Spanish inns it is the essential minimum and to be regarded partly as disinfectant, partly as anaesthetic.

Leaning over the back of my chair, the boy examined me, in broadest Andaluz, as to what I had seen and done in Arcos. He was anxious that none of the splendours of his *pueblo* should be missed and inquired particularly if I had yet seen the "ca'tishu" where an old English lady lived alone. I begged him to explain himself, which he did by repeating the word over and over again very slowly and loudly. At last, in despair at this impenetrable dullness, he seized my notebook and pencil and drew in some detail an ancient, ramparted castle, writing the word CASTILLO underneath in block letters in case his meaning were not yet clear. But of course! How very dense of me. Beaming, he added a few touches to his picture. At this moment the proprietress came in and the youth appealed for her support. She agreed at once it would be unthinkable to leave Arcos without paying the lady a visit. She was English: she was very rich; and she lived all alone. She would be delighted.

But what did she do with herself all day long?

"Nothing! As I say, she is rich," the proprietress explained.

For the life of me I could not see why this lady should receive visitors merely because they chose to call, for there seemed no purpose in living behind such fine, solid doors if they were then to be thrown open so lightly; but to content the eager pair and because there was something attractively mysterious in the situation of this compatriot—one of the splendid host of English eccentrics, perhaps, who do so much to enliven the globe—I panted and sweated up the hill for a third time that day. Nothing venture, nothing win: suppose the lady stayed indoors all day for fear that someone should call while she was out? And I began to picture her, rising tall and gracious to throw a log on the fire as she rang for buttered muffins.

But the castle looked as impregnable as castle could and there was not a sign of British life about it, not even a Union Jack or a pack of hounds. The ancient bell I pulled gave out a hollow, grudging note as if it preferred on the whole that people did not touch it. At last very slowly and creakily the gate opened an inch or two and a woman's face looked severely through the crack. No, the *señora* could see no one. The *señora* never saw anyone. No, the castle was not to be shown. It was never shown to anyone. Slowly the gate creaked to again. It was what I expected and as I deserved, and the exclusive chatelaine had my fullest approval and sympathy.

In one of the narrow lanes that led to the *castillo* there now appeared an enormous American motor car driving the oncoming mules and carts backwards before it and causing the inhabitants to leap to the wall for safety. It was followed in reverent silence by a little crowd of boys and men. As I came up it stopped, and a round head covered with straw-coloured bristles poked out of a window.

"Hey! You're not Spanish."

The head went on to explain that it had seen the Church of Santa Maria, which was pretty though, it guessed, not really worth the ride from Jerez, and inquired what else it ought to see before turning round. Hopefully I indicated the *castillo*, but the head guessed it didn't care for crumby old castles; it wanted Art. But I was a stranger there myself. Then the head withdrew for consultation with another head, shaped like an egg this time and as smooth, and once more emerged.

"Hey! We're going on back to Jerez. Don't you want to ride with us?"

A handsome offer, and gratefully accepted, for there were still a couple of hours before the bus would leave and I was beginning to feel like something left in the oven. The car squeezed its way to the Plaza de España, where there was room to turn for the descent of the hill: the Americans having introduced themselves as Bill and Joe, we crept off down the lane again with the driver giving way now and again to exasperated comment.

"Why don't they widen the Goddamn street?"

"Wake up, Sambo! Want me to run you down?"

The pair were interesting as the first Americans, except for holiday-makers, that I had come across on my journey. To hear some Spaniards talk, you would fancy the country was under an American occupation; and the supplement of a New York paper I had seen in London, devoted to the wonderful job that was being done there, had led me to fear the worst. But the Americans in Spain turned out to be much like the churches burned in the Civil War, seldom or never where you happened to be, although thick as flies (it would be asserted) in territory some way off. But here at last were Bill and Joe, engaged on work so vital to the preservation of Western values that they could not bring themselves to divulge its nature, beyond darkly stating they were at present on Survey.

At the foot of the hill there was a café and Bill guessed we better have a drink, since it would be all of thirty-five minutes before we could get another. The place was empty at this hour except for two youths who were buying a bottle of cordial and another, smaller one which contained a dark fluid obviously potent. "Hey, Sambo, kay esta?" genially shouted Bill, and explained then to me it was his habit to talk to everyone he met, so that he could get the feel of the country. Smiling, the youth offered him the bottle in the graceful Spanish invitation which is not meant to be taken up, any more than the English "How do you do?" calls for details of our physical condition. Bill took the bottle and, pouring himself a liberal dose, drank it down, pulling a face as he did so. "Lemme," said Joe, and repeated the performance. Mournfully, the boys watched their little Sunday treat dwindling away.

"Go on. Take some. You'll hurt their feelings," Bill urged me.

"Ugh! We better have some brandy quick and take the Goddamn taste away," said Joe.

On the way back to Jerez, as their beautiful car sailed over the bumpy road, they discussed with good-humoured toleration the shortcomings of the Spanish race, its discourtesy, savagery, sloth, inefficiency and, in particular, its failure to appreciate the United States.

That evening the fountain played in the Square of the Catholic Rulers because it was Sunday.

"*Simpatica, la fuente, no?*" the waiter asked.

The word was well chosen. It was indeed *simpatica* to see how the precious water was squandered. The part that water, or the lack of it, plays in the life of Spaniards can hardly be exaggerated. It is a favourite topic of conversation, like the weather in England; the people of Madrid would formerly argue the merits of their two water systems as a constant theme, and a good approach to a stranger whom you wish to draw out is to ask about the water in the *pueblo*, a matter on which he will hold forth with fluency. Fierce passions are roused, the most relentless village feuds begun, by someone taking more than his due share of the supply of irrigation. But to make the Sunday evening more pleasant, the noble people of Jerez de la Frontera were throwing it into the air as gaily and nonchalantly as if they lived in the Lake District, or still had the Moors to teach them how to look after it.

"*Muy simpatica,*" I agreed. He watched it a little while longer, smiling to himself, and then went to fetch my beer. Fifteen minutes elapsed and then he came back with it: another fifteen, and he brought olives and anchovies.

"It all takes time," he explained.

There was a bond between us because the evening before he

had dropped a key in the dark and I had helped him to find it: so easily are good relations established in Andalusia.

It was about eight o'clock and the town, in all its finery, was strolling up and down the square under the stolid palm trees with purple climbers hugging their stems. Everyone had put on a brave show, down to the babies in arms who in spotless muslin and silk sashes looked as if they had just been snipped off a Christmas tree. The town had a fine air of patrician calm about it, and a flavour of the nineteenth century. Now and again an elegant carriage and pair would go bowling by, driven by a liveried coachman with confident ease as if he were unaware that other means of travel had yet been thought of. Whole families were piling into the town *fiacres*, lugubriously hooded and drawn by feeble, despondent horses; or a solitary rider would make his way through the crowded place on a high-stepping Andalusian mount.

A more contemporary note was struck by a cinema near at hand, whose loudspeaker was blaring its head off although the doors would not open for another hour. The poster announcing the Hollywood film to be shown that night had a sticker on it marked "Authorized for Adults" and it was discouraging to see, therefore, that nobody in the queue looked more than fourteen years old. With immense, self-sacrificing care a sort of clerical watch committee views all the films and classifies them in appropriate groups (Forbidden to All, Authorized for Adults of Sound Moral Education Only, Authorized for All Adults, Tolerated, Permitted to All, etc.), and it is a grievous thing that many young people should regard its work merely as a guide to the more rewarding entertainments.

All at once in the square three youths came bounding along, followed by a troop of little boys, all shouting and laughing and panting with excitement. One of them had a wounded swallow in his hand, and this he threw into the air like a paper dart, when it went a little way, faltered and dropped to the earth.

After it tore the gang to snatch it up and hurl it again, round and round the gardens. Sometimes the youth would vary the entertainment by tossing it up and down and catching it like a ball, while it fluttered and cheeped in his hand. No one displayed anything but a sweet indifference except when the little creature fell on a bed of flowers and a keeper hurried forward with lifted stick to complain of the boys trampling over it.

In Spain it often happens at the very moment when one feels most admiring and appreciative that some incident of the kind will intervene to shatter the mood. No people should be so magnificent and so repulsive at once. The horrid impression now was created less by the action of the youths, for there are cruel boys anywhere, than by the acquiescence of the public at large. Nothing was more illuminating: and there came into my mind, as contrast, a to-do of the evening before. Passing the lovely old Church of San Miguel I had dropped in for a moment, although my veil was at home and the usual notice was up in the porch about the modesty expected of the Christian Woman. In one of the chapels Benediction was just being said and everyone turned eagerly round for a good look at the newcomer. At the sight of my bare head a little wave of agitation swept over the worshippers, like a breeze passing over a field of corn. Flustered whispering took place: people gesticulated reproachfully towards their own coverings: a little miss of eighteen or so jumped up from her knees and came to me with a handkerchief in her hand which she shook commandingly in front of my eyes. The air was full of disapproval and hostility, the attention of the entire assembly switched from their devotions to me; and to avoid causing further distress I went away. A small infringement of custom was profoundly troubling to the popular mind: the torment of a helpless little bird left it unmoved.

I paid for the beer and went away for a quiet walk in the country. In a few minutes Jerez was left behind and under a fiery sunset a sweep of bare, tawny hills went rolling away as far as the eye could see. White cabins were dotted about in the folds of them and as darkness began to fall their little lights came out and merrily twinkled. Each side of the winding dusty paths the round spiky leaves of the prickly pear turned black against a sky of Persian green. Not a sound was to be heard but the cicadas twanging away in their thickets like so many diminutive guitars or the distant barking of a dog. Very few people were still about, a grizzled countryman returning from the fields, girls setting out for the town, two women trotting along on one mule. A great peace lay over those wide dusky spaces, and at last I went tranquilly home by the light of the stars to a pitiless Spanish dinner and an implacable Spanish bed.

6

IN THE MORNING I was awakened by the merry hum of a market which had established itself in the plaza outside the hotel. Beautiful water-jars of classic form and baked of pale clay, many of a size to hold a small child, were arranged in orderly rows while here and there, comfortably propped against the larger ones, a vendor slept. Women swarmed about the wheelbarrows piled with tomatoes and eggs or haggled amiably for little bunches of flowers. Terrified hens peered out of the wicker baskets in which they were compressed or lay on the ground in heaps, tied leg to leg. A pure white mule stepped delicately through the rubbish on the ground with a pannier of white daisies swaying on each side of its back. The air was full of the vivacious greetings of Spaniards who have not met each other for twenty-four hours, and of laughter and friendly altercation.

In the hotel itself, although it was long after nine, all was peace and quiet: the night watchman, still on duty, dozed by the switchboard. I took coffee at the bar of a nearby café in company with a number of men, grave and preoccupied as senators, all of whom were beginning their day with a glass of brandy. About a yard from where I stood was a basin with running water fixed to the wall, and here a magnificent old countryman, with high cheekbones and side-whiskers under his stiff Andalusian hat, was apparently washing his hands; but when I turned for a better look at him I saw that in fact he was relieving himself. The immense dignity, the utter unconcern, with which he performed this necessary act in a crowded public room left a most favourable impression.

When breakfast was over, I went to visit one or two of the sherry lodges. The first was a small one, with the pleasant family air of long-established concerns, and stood in beautiful grounds with trim grass and gay beds of flowers. On one of the chimneys a stork perched on one leg, guarding her nest with the peculiar air of importance that storks always have at such times: an importance all the more comical since, as the guide informed me, she had built her nest so incompetently that they had pushed a support underneath it to save the eggs from falling down the chimney.

This guide was a man of vivid personality who used the English tongue in a most original way. Much of his spare time, he told me, was spent in studying it. He had a romantic passion for the England he had never seen, which he thought must be due to a drop of English blood from an ancestor. He showed everything there was, the presses and the special nailed shoes for treading the grapes and the great casks piled one on the other in the *criaderos* or nurseries awaiting their time to enter the *solera*, all ranged in high, airy barns; but fascinating as his information was, or such of it as I could understand, more pleasing still was the lovely joy and pride he took in it all, his sense of the absolute worth of what was being done. His eye glowed with an inward light as he spoke of the great wines slowly maturing here before they went forth to ease the pains of humanity: his vocabulary, his idiom, grew richer and stranger yet: the most miserable teetotaller alive must have yielded in time to the warmth of his persuasion and I, an old believer, was entirely carried away by it.

This happy confidence is to be found in all the *bodegas* of Jerez and spills over into their printed advertisements, which become little hymns of devotion and praise. "Sherry! Joy to the sorrowful, strength to the weak!" will run the preamble to a list of types and prices and there is true feeling in it, far removed from the synthetic enthusiasm of other manufacturers. It is difficult to read unmoved the booklet on sherry published by Jerez Industrial, of whose flavour the following passage may give some idea:

"*Fino: the colour of sunlight: 'topaz' is the metaphor used since 1836. Tastes of almonds. Pungent aroma. Fino Sherry is so sensitive that it responds to the arrival of Spring even in the bottle. On its surface appears the tenuous yeast-like flor, in other words, the wine flowers as though it still had roots in the vineyard: indeed, the experts say that the appearance of this 'flower' occurs at the precise time when the mother vine first puts out green shoots. This must be Nature's most involved and romantic love-call!*"

Similar phrases were tripping off the tongue of my companion one after the other. The tour ended in a gay little private bar where stood a row of bottles which visitors are welcome, and indeed expected, to sample one after the other: it is seldom they leave the premises in the same condition as they enter. Having another call to make I contented myself with one glass only: for such is the power of this glorious liquid that, given a chance, it gently expunges all thought of duty and purpose, focusing the mind instead on the delights of meditation and the importance of inactivity.

It was fortunate that I did so, for at the next place of call things were differently managed. This one was Gonzalez Byass which, with Domecq, is the largest and most important of the sixty-two lodges in Jerez. The visit opened quietly: I had no personal introduction here and was asked to fill out a form, much as if I were trying to see a Civil Servant in London. After a wait of some time in a formidably businesslike room, a spare, melancholy gentleman appeared and announced in a fading voice that he was ready to take me round. Once again I saw the presses, the *criaderos*, the machines for bottling, corking, ticketing, while the guide sadly explained their uses or delivered a lecture on the history of the firm. I was on the point of begging him to desist and to unburden himself instead of the private sorrow which seemed to weigh upon him when we came to a barn in which were stored great casks of wine ready matured, and here we were joined by a man with a long, slender pipe in his hand.

"Tio Pepe," said the guide dismally, halting in front of one of the casks and signalling to the man with the pipe.

Quick as lightning, he plunged it into the butt, filled two glasses and stepped back to watch the effect they made. I took this to be the culmination of the tour and, handing back the empty glass, turned vaguely in the direction of the door.

"This way, please!" said the guide. He walked on a few paces and stopped in front of another cask. "Apostoles," he said, signalling. Again the glasses were filled and emptied and the guide, now showing a few early signs of animation, seemed distressed that I would not have another. "You should have taken more of the Tio Pepe perhaps; English people always seem to prefer the dry," he mused.

"Matusalem," he said a few moments later, and signalled.

In this instructive and enlivening fashion we toured the cellar and at each brief halt the spirits of the guide rose a little higher. By the time we had crowned the varied succession of *copita*s with a glass of Insuperable brandy, he was as gay as a lark. Sherry was the answer that never failed. Visitors came, serious people from all over the world, asking factual questions and making notes in little books, only to leave treading on air and laughing like children. Once, indeed, an American lady had arrived at ten in the morning and never opened her mouth except to swallow four glasses of the Insuperable one after the other before departing, speechless and immovable to the end, but that experience was never repeated. Within these walls, he told me, a note of reverence creeping into his voice, grief and pain were left behind. At this moment I was overcome by a fit of coughing and he rushed me back to the Insuperable barrel. It was the one sure remedy in such cases. In fact, the best cure for a cough, and one much used by Spaniards, was four fingers of brandy and one of hot coffee in a glass: he got me to repeat this after him to make certain I had the proportions right:

"Cuatro *dedos de coñac*. Un *dedo de café!*"

Through a golden haze I inspected the notable sights that remained. There was a circular grange built by Eiffel to house the famous *solera* of 1847 with the *escudos* of the Spanish provinces and of foreign countries painted on the butts: the collection of casks dedicated to the great or autographed by them in white chalk; the museum of dusty, cobwebbed casks dating from the foundation of 1835: and many other curious and interesting things of which, alas! my relaxed and contented brain failed to make a proper note and for which later on I searched my memory in vain.

In one of the granges were twelve plump barrels of Olorosa named each after an apostle, and in the middle of them a giant one for Christ Himself: El Cristo del Gran Poder, perhaps. The habit Spaniards have of naming their good things in this way is an attractive one, showing a truly grateful and pious spirit, and the expressions on the guide's face as he gazed devotedly upon the casks was beautiful to see. As in the first *bodega*, here too was the sense of people dedicated to the service of mankind: here too the family atmosphere, the smiling workmen, the well-kept gardens where Tio Pepe, a little white donkey, gravely drew his cart down the path; and here the same warm and generous welcome to the stranger. With one last lyrical flight the guide, whose now beaming face paid sherry a tribute more eloquent than any words could do, left me at the gates.

The walk home was a curious affair. Although the sun beat down as fiercely as ever the sky was strangely overcast and threatening, and I called out to a peasant riding by on a mule that it looked like thundery weather. He replied oddly, with a loud laugh, by asking if I had enjoyed the *bodegas*.

Yes; but what had that to do with it?

"You have your sun-glasses on," he explained and, still guffawing, rode away.

I snatched them off in confusion. On the impressive walls of the Alcazar was a notice to young people to refrain, out of respect for culture, from throwing stones at them: just now a bunch of girls and boys were stoning away with all their might and for some reason it seemed divinely witty of them. I stood there feebly laughing and, when they stared, unwisely attempted to share the joke: at which they stared all the harder and I was forced to conclude they had no sense of humour. After I had gone some way it occurred to me that I had addressed them in French, but I decided against going back. Not content with reeling to and fro, the houses and buildings had a subtly altered appearance, deliberately misleading as I thought, and in no time I was lost in a tangle of lanes and alleys until at last I stumbled on the Calle Pérez Galdós: where the contrast between the miserable street named for Spain's greatest novelist and those grandiose avenues all over the country called after a certain fat adventurer plunged me into a sudden, deep woe. Indeed, I was on the point of tears; but then it struck me that I was simply drunk. Pig drunk in the middle of the day and in full view of respectable Spanish families. Those sherry-makers lured honest people into their caves and gave them a lot of fine talk about involved and romantic love-calls, and all the while they were scheming to make them tipsy and send them out to act the buffoon. My face now working indignantly, I hailed a *fiacre* and drove to Los Cisnes for the largest, most solid meal that money could buy. *Gazpacho* there was, cold as a mountain lake, with dishes of bread, onion, pimiento and cucumber to throw in it, an Algerian omelet, roasted sucking-pig, a great bowl of figs, apricots and cherries and splendid Turkish coffee, for less than ten shillings. A little steadied, I went home and floated, or possibly flew, up the stairs to bed and slept until ten in the evening.

7

THE ROAD from Jerez to Seville ran through cornlands that
stretched away in a vast yellow steppe, broken here and there
by a spine of tall, dark eucalyptus: through fields and groves of
olive, and prairies where horsemen drove great herds of sleek
cattle. Now and then against the horizon a village sharply and
briefly appeared, topping its hill as Spanish villages do, unlike
our own which nestle in hollows: otherwise all was undulating
plainland, already at this early hour quivering under the terrible
blaze. It was in this country and this weather that St. Teresa, in
her thick wool habit, refreshed herself by meditating on the
souls in Purgatory.

While the menfolk sat in conclave under trees or slept, the
women were hard at work on the land, dressed for greater
freedom of movement in trousers over which, for the sake of
modesty, they wore ample skirts as well. As a protection against
the sun all had swathed their heads and necks with thick white
linen cloths under the broad grass hats, from which their hot
faces glowed forth like burning coals. Merely to look at them
turned one almost giddy with heat, but they laboured on with a
will, pausing only to give an encouraging wave of the hand as
the coach went by. The spontaneous, unresentful greeting to
people luckier than themselves was touching and very Spanish.

Men do occasionally work as well and in fact we came on a

party of them at it. Some were digging out earth from the side of the road and shovelling it into panniers on mules, decorated with gay crimson tassels. When the panniers were full, they led the mules a little way off and tipped it out again. Others were slowly and thoughtfully stirring cauldrons of tar with long wooden staves. Still others were spreading tar and broken flints on the road and beating them in with implements that looked like a croquet mallet. A charming air of leisure hung over it all, a sense of energies prudently husbanded; and a notice near by said it was part of a scheme for the modernization of the district, decreed by the Public Works Office in Seville.

On arriving at the city, I went as usual with the first tout who spoke and had no reason at all to regret it. He led me to a *pension* unlike any I ever encountered in Spain before or since. A wonderfully suburban daintiness was the note, from the flowered silks of the "hostess" to the lampshades of frilly paper in the bedroom. The parlour was furnished with leather chairs and sofa of pastel green, with backs of cream lace and cream fringes, and on the wall were a number of English prints: *The Old Homestead, The Thatcher, Horses in a Stable* and *The Warreners*. At mealtime one sparrow's portion of food followed another, tastefully served as in Ann's Pantry on tables that were rather too small, and for each guest there was one tiny glass of wine, as Spanish law decrees; and to have raised the matter of a replenishment in that refined atmosphere would somehow have been unthinkable. The clients were mainly English ladies who frequently expressed delight at finding such homelike surroundings in foreign parts. The only Spanish features in the place were the voice of the owner, a voice of such sustained power and resonance that the very air seemed to go on humming after she had completed her say, and the wireless which was left roaring on at the top of its lungs all day in competition. At first I thought the whole thing conceived deliberately with an eye to visitors from Wimbledon and Welwyn

Garden City; but the *pension* was a large flat near the top of a modern apartment house and, as my room looked onto the well, I was able to see into other, similar flats all the way down, furnished every one with the same horrifying prettiness. Each hall door was fitted with a medallion of the Sacred Heart as well as a spy-hole through which the arrivals and departures of other tenants could be observed.

My only purpose in coming to Seville, at this time of year both much too hot and much too full of foreigners, was to ask our Consul if I would be given permission to visit the copper mines at Rio Tinto; and he, after kindly making inquiries, was able to assure me in no time at all that it was out of the question. This was not unexpected, for the Spanish authorities are apparently convinced that any foreigner who wants to see more than cathedrals, *fiestas* and bull-fights is a spy, and very likely a Red into the bargain. This mania of theirs may perhaps be due to a sense of their backwardness in material things compared with the rest of Europe, and to their dread of ridicule, as keen now as in the days of Richard Ford. Two attitudes arise out of it, one bovine and sulky, a take-it-or-leave-it-but-preferably-leave-it, and the other of absurd touchiness, which can land the stranger in uncomfortable situations. Recently in Cadiz some English people had been arrested by an Army officer for photographing a group of children as they danced in the street. The children were dirty and ragged, and the officer said the photographer's purpose could only be to belittle and humiliate Spain. From this he went on to declare that they were probably spies as well, taking pictures of the harbour works and fortifications; and he handed them over to the police to sit in a Spanish jail until all the films they had used so far had been developed. The whole business took some little time, during which it must be feared that the officer's real duties were not attended to.

On receiving the Consul's report, I made ready to leave the next morning, and spent the rest of the day wandering at a snail's pace through the gardens and lanes of this delectable city. The sun made my thin blouse feel like a sheet of flame and the rims of my sunglasses burned my face as in some mediaeval torture. Everywhere was a flutter of fans and weary voices exclaiming at the heat. *Ay Dios, que calor!* The Spaniards resign themselves to their climate no more than we to ours. Under the ceiling of foliage in the Alameda a youth joyously wielded the municipal hose, the great sparkling jet of water narrowly missing cars, pedestrians and mules, the spray falling with a delicious sound on the baking stones; and in no time all was as dry as a bone once more. But as refuge there was always the Cathedral, into whose enormous twilit interior I ever and again would thankfully plunge, as into a pool.

Hard by the Cathedral was the Archbishop's Palace. Today there was none of the swift to and fro of plump black figures, the muttered consultations, the hand-kissings ordinarily to be seen at the doors of such a place. The windows were shuttered and the courtyard bare and the very building seemed to wear an expression implacable and defiant. Inside lay Cardinal Segura, old and ill, but stubborn as ever, refusing either to retire to a monastery as the Vatican had decreed or to receive the new Archbishop appointed in his place.

The rise to power of this interesting, perverse old man had been as notable as his fall, if fall be the word for a state of affairs which he so positively declined to accept. In a miserably poor and barren region of the province of Salamanca lived, or existed, some people known as the Hurdes, undersized, goitrous and often half-witted, who ate berries and roots and lived in holes in the ground. They are still there at the present time but their conditions have greatly improved, thanks in the first place to Alfonso XIII and more recently to the Church. King Alfonso had read of them in Chapman and Buck's *Unexplored Spain* and, much distressed, went down to the region to see for himself; and, as Segura was then priest of a parish in the neighbour-

61

hood, the King sent a message that he wanted to speak to him at once. Father Segura, however, sent back word that he was too busy to come. Kings, unlike dictators, seem to enjoy this kind of talk; at all events the two of them soon became friends and in the course of time Segura was raised to the Primacy.

With General Franco his relations were less happy; and this has earned him the approval of some people who may not realize that one cause of friction has been the Caudillo's refusal to persecute Protestants as actively as the Cardinal would have liked. Indeed, he has made no secret of his wish to see the Holy Office restored to its function in Spain. To the gay, life-loving people of Seville, this gloomy fanatic, a true thirteenth-century figure, was even less acceptable. He forbade them to dance: it was like forbidding the Welsh to sing or the English to go to football matches. It is a grim conception of the religious life that he has, unyielding and absolute and entirely Spanish, as Spanish as his own megalomania.

Some idea of this last is to be gained from the monument he put up to the Sacred Hearts of Jesus and Mary on a hill some way beyond the city across the river. He erected it in 1942, a time when the land was still suffering terrible distress after the Civil War, and it cost millions of pesetas. It is a vulgar and pretentious piece of work. A figure of the Virgin stands near the foot of the hill with the words MARIA PURISIMA in huge white letters laid out like a warning to aircraft, while Stations of the Cross go up through gardens each side to an open-air temple at the summit, over which towers a figure of Christ some twenty-five feet high pointing to his Sacred Heart and gazing out towards the slums of Seville: the whole executed something in the wedding-cake tradition of the Sacré Cœur in Paris. But the cream of the thing, and, one suspects, its *raison d'être*, is the stately mausoleum below, in which in the fullness of time the Cardinal proposed to be buried. It is a fine example of what results when continual and intimate association with the Most High has led to a confusion of identity.

For the moment, however, the Cardinal still was with us, braving the Holy See and the Spanish authorities both, to the scandal and amusement of Christendom.

Incidentally, he is not the only man in Seville who has the answer to everything. Here, in the very shadow of his robe as it were, labours an Irish Protestant Mission, struggling against the tides of Popery much as a child might attempt to push the sea back with a wooden spade. The remark of Mendizabal to Borrow comes to mind: "What a strange infatuation is this which drives you over lands and waters with Bibles in your hands!" We must wait for Judgment Day perhaps to know if "infatuation" is the word or not: what is certain now is that the endeavours of these honest people are intensely irritating to Spaniards, who feel themselves put on a level with the heathen of Africa and who say, with some justice, that they might be equally well employed at home. Their few conversions only cause trouble in the families concerned, provoking dissension and disharmony, social and political embarrassment. But no one is so ruthless as the crusading religious, be he Protestant, Catholic or anything else.

Although the copper mines were not to be seen, I kept to my plan of visiting Huelva, on the bay from which Columbus set sail and the last big Spanish town before the Portuguese border. On the way to it we crossed the Rio Tinto, at this time of year a shrunken stream moving sluggishly between violent red banks, its waters touched with the purple and green iridescence of burnished copper. We also passed through the pretty little village of La Niebla, where once had lived a most original and ingenious Englishwoman. She had taken a passionate interest in the locality, holding indeed some rather fanciful theories about it, and she had left behind her a private museum, now utterly neglected in the Spanish way and not easy of access, as the key to it was always alleged to be missing.

As soon as we got to Huelva I went to Punta de Umbria for a swim. It took about an hour to reach it by a small, grunting steamer whose decks were weighed almost down to water-level by the holiday crowd aboard and which tacked uncertainly through the creeks and channels of the delta between banks covered with bright green grass and umbrella pines. The beach was a good one with miles of yellow sand, and plenty of bathing-huts and places for refreshment. It was also entirely Spanish, as could be seen from the modest bathing-dresses of the women and the general gravity of deportment: the noise of a similar resort in Italy would have been ear-splitting. The most animated people there were the fathers who hugged and kissed their children, delighting in them and worshipping them, in contrast to northern men, who in the presence of their families usually have a harassed and even a faintly ridiculous air.

The season here opens about mid-July, when the waters are blessed, after which the older people hasten to take the customary fifteen baths of the year one after the other. The younger ones no longer restrict themselves in this way: in fact the foreign habit of immersion is noticeably taking hold of the country. No one swam very much, as it was necessary to wade out a couple of hundred yards before there was water deep enough, but they gambolled innocently in the shallows or crowded under umbrellas on the beach to escape from the sun.

In the afternoon I set out for La Rábida, the monastery where Columbus made his calculations for the venture across the Atlantic and where he spent his last night before sailing. Having dallied too long on the shore, I missed the bus from Huelva to the ferry and had to spend thirty pesetas on a taxi, only to find on arrival that the ferry had gone as well and there would not be another for two hours. The taxi-driver, with the gallantry of his kind, and also its belief that foreigners are unable to shift for themselves, harangued a group of men on the shore in the endeavour to get me a private boat; but none of them wished to interrupt his afternoon's repose. At last he felt he must really go back and drive his taxi once more, but he did not like to seem as if he were leaving me in the lurch; and he therefore pretended that a small vessel just leaving the opposite shore was in truth a ferry, mysteriously added to the time-table for this single occasion. The fact that it was steaming off in the other direction he explained by the strength of the currents, which made it impossible for any but the largest ship to come straight across.

"*Cinco minutos!*" he cried encouragingly and, leaping into his taxi, drove off. Hopefully I watched the little craft dart hither and thither through the shoals for half an hour until it was swallowed up in the distance. Then I resigned myself and spent the time until the ferry came in staring over the estuary at the white walls of the monastery, and in contemplation of the memorial to Christopher Columbus that had been put up by an American lady. It showed a huge, formless figure emerging partly from a column and partly from a great rough cross: round the pedestal were engraved Red Indians and other typical figures. The symbolism inclined to obscurity, but the stress seemed to fall rather on the marvel of America being discovered than on the triumph of Columbus in crossing unknown seas: while from the shadowy folds that cowled the monster's head peered forth the simple features of any G.I., turned steadfastly westwards.

La Rábida was very well worth waiting for. We sat in the little ferry and watched the wide stretch of blue water melt into the blue sky, dancing and shimmering in the way that makes a trip in southern seas so delightful. It steered past mudflats dried and caked with salt, with sea-lavender and sea-thistle growing out of them, to the landing-stage; and here a little thin smiling Franciscan, with a last hilarious fling at the ferry-master, took charge of me and led the way up through an avenue of palms to the monastery, chattering gaily as he went. He told me he knew America intimately, by which he meant Boliva, and urged me to lose no time in visiting it. I asked him what nationality Columbus was, as I understood the Italians had views of their own on the subject, and he shot me a beady glance from his dancing black eyes.

"As far as I am concerned, he was Spanish," he said.

He went on to regale me with stories of the great man's life, some of them very tall indeed; but I had received warning along the way that there was a humorist of no mean order in the fraternity. At the monastery gate he handed me over to another smiling Franciscan on the grounds that he spoke English, although this was not supported by the evidence. Four Brothers lived here and cared for the place, but only one more appeared this afternoon, a gaunt wild-looking individual who, with his habit tucked up about his waist, was feverishly using a feather-duster in one of the rooms.

Columbus spent six years in this place while he made his studies and worked out his plans for the great venture. His bare little cell was there as he had left it, the room where he had had his conferences with the two Franciscans who advised him, the chapel with the image in alabaster of Our Lady before which he and his sailors prayed at the moment of setting forth. There were models of each of the three ships that sailed, the *Pinta*, the *Santa Maria* and the *Niña*, or Child, that had only eighteen men aboard. In one room hung the flags of the Spanish States of America, with a casket of earth from each, in filial tribute: the benign faces of Ferdinand and Isabel the Catholic looked down from the walls of another. Much of the place is just as it was at the time of Columbus: the old *clausura* looks today as it did to the pilgrims who used it once as their inn; and where replacements or imitations have had to be made the work has been done with taste and skill. The Brother explained everything with the greatest pride and joy, taking care that not one item of the repository in his charge should be passed by. Now and again he would run to a window and point over the monastery gardens with their palms and geraniums and oleanders to the great panorama of the Rio Tinto and the massed blue hills away towards the Portuguese frontier, fifty or sixty miles off; and with his arm fraternally round my neck would feast his own eyes on the magnificent picture as if he could never enjoy it enough.

In the entrance-hall a notice said the monastery entreated visitors to give them alms. I had only fifteen pesetas in change and some hundred-peseta notes; and one of these with a sharp inward pang I handed over. But the pain of it vanished at once before the intense delight on the Brother's face, a delight which he made no attempt to conceal. He took the note and pored over it, he waved it joyously in the air exclaiming, "God will repay this!" he patted me lovingly on the back and urged me to take wine. Then he trotted away out of sight and presently a Brother bounded from the monastery and down the hill with a shopping-bag on his arm. I hoped he was going to lay in some groceries, for they all looked as if a square meal would do them no harm. And when the Brother came back and saw me off, fluttering his fingers in the attractively babyish farewell of the country, I wished the gift had been a spontaneous one: the beauty of the place and its moving associations as well as the kindness and simplicity of the Friars made it seem a poor enough return.

Time had passed meanwhile without my noticing it, and the last ferry had gone. I had to charter a private boat, and I expected to walk the five miles to Huelva, as the last bus had theoretically gone as well. But one of those Spanish miracles intervened and an unexplained bus stood under the trees on the farther shore. It was just about to leave, but stopped when I bawled to it from midstream, blowing its horn impatiently more than once to make it clear that the whole thing was an imposition, but still bravely waiting. But the boatman had no change. Nobody in Spain ever has any change, because nobody has any money. I asked him to run and get some and he said, Where? Where? The bus honked severely and growled with its engine. So I ran to the conductor, who grumbled and scolded, snatched the note from my hand, advanced the boatman's wage from his fare-money, stopped the bus at the first café on the road, changed my note after loud altercation, recouped himself for the loan, took my fare, explained each transaction slowly and loudly as to someone mentally handicapped, and in a voice that apparently shook with rage, and then, when all at last was tidied up, gave me a broad gold-toothed smile of forgiveness; and seating himself at my side entertained me the whole way back to Huelva.

8

THE BELLS of Spanish churches have a distinctive note, at once deep and hollow like that of a metal drum and tinny like the clatter of pokers and tongs. They also are contentious; an outcry from one is immediately and angrily taken up by another down the road. The argument begins early in the morning and continues gradually dying down until noon.

Awakened at six o'clock by a furious burst from the neighbouring *parroquia*, I got up and went out. People were spreading their wares along the sides of the road. There were baskets of tiny white eggs, mountains of garlic and pumpkins, waxy green lemons and miserable, shrunken cherries and strawberries. Blind lottery-ticket sellers already shuffled about chanting *"Suerte! Suerte!"* in dull mechanical voices as if the word could have no charm for such as they. A young Gypsy sat on the pavement edge and crooned to her baby, as filthy as she and marked heavily with a disease of the skin. At this time of day the well-fed and well-clothed are still asleep and the poor have the streets to themselves; and more horrifyingly visible than ever are the army of deformed or maimed, the blind, legless, dwarfed and hunchbacked. At every turn of the eye a reminder of life's cruelty rises up: a sense of the tragedy underlying all things in this land forces itself on the spectator, however indifferent or calloused he may be.

In a little workman's café, whose walls were covered with portraits of bull-fighters cut out of magazines and pasted up, I asked for an *espresso con leche*. The owner started to prepare it, but at that moment a man came in and the pair at once fell into a warm discussion of the merits of various stars of the ring. The owner would be on the point of fixing the coffee under the steam when something further would strike him and, laying it down, he would dart off and wag a finger in the other man's face. He did this several times, and then made the coffee at last, but the whole performance had to be repeated with the milk. Sallies burst from the lips of both like the cackle of competing machine-guns and I began to despair of my breakfast. When it finally came the conversation dropped immediately and was followed by dead silence.

I asked if any of the fighters whose pictures were on the wall came from the locality. At once the proprietor's eye kindled and he burst into his machine-gun rattle again. No, none of these, but Litri, the great Litri, the greatest of them all, he was a son of Huelva. The bravest sword, the finest artist! None like him since Belmonte! A giant!

I thought he had retired.

"Retired!" shrieked the owner. "Litri retired!"

"*Café solo,*" said a Guardia Civil, who had just come in.

No doubt I thought Litri had retired. Many people thought many things. Many people said he had lost his nerve. But they didn't say it in Huelva. Litri had made so much money he didn't fight often nowadays. He was still the greatest of them all. A millionaire several times over!

"*Café solo,*" said the Guardia Civil.

Had I seen Litri's house? It was not far away, here for all to see. The house of a nobleman. His mother lived in it with him. He never moved to Seville or Madrid, but honoured the town of his birth. Look, I should see that house. Here the proprietor snatched up a piece of paper and drew a picture of the house and a plan for getting to it.

"*Café solo!*" said the Guardia Civil.

Better still, I should see Litri in the ring. It was worth waiting years. No one ever forgot it. I must read the papers every day to see when Litri was fighting. On no account should I leave Spain before.

I had seen Litri fight.

"Then," said the owner, calming down at once, "you know what I mean."

"*Oiga!*" roared the Guardia Civil. "*Café solo!*"

The owner looked at him in astonishment. "*Hombre!*" he said. "I am not a mile away." And with the unhurried movements of a man well within his rights he made the policeman's coffee.

How pleasant a thing this Spanish enthusiasm is! and how limp, rain-washed and colourless it makes the northerner feel. No one here is neutral, balanced, objective, fair or "responsible," qualities possibly to be esteemed but arising from the absence of passion. The special note in the proprietor's voice as he uttered the name "Litri" was beautiful to hear. And Huelva, ah, Huelva! It was a big dirty port with a maze of shabby streets. The shops were uninviting and the cafés without charm. Down on the quays the cork, roughly cut in the factories, was piled like thousands of bath-mats, gutted fish hung on lines to dry like clothes on the peg, outside the fishermen's cabins a wilderness of old brown nets draped from their poles: hungry dogs and cats slunk warily about and the gutters were full of refuse. Or so the cold eye of a stranger saw it, but to a man of glowing inward vision like the owner of this little bar it was the fountain of all excellence and cradle of the great, who naturally preferred it to Seville or Madrid.

In the afternoon I went on by coach to Aracena, a beautiful

place little visited by foreigners but a favourite holiday resort for the well-to-do of the region. Perhaps because Aracena was off the tourist route, the coach provided was not one of the shiny monsters with comfortable numbered seats but a kind of Noah's Ark into which the passengers crammed themselves as best they could. Everyone seemed to know everyone else, and the conductor was such a favourite all along the road that there was difficulty in collecting him up after each pause. The driver, on the other hand, was a saturnine individual who rounded his huge silent back over the wheel as, puffing at a cigar, he urged his vehicle rapidly up the steep mountain roads and round the hairpin bends with a sheer drop awaiting us on either side should he ever miscalculate.

It was splendid country again. About half an hour from Huelva the road begins to climb, at first through gently rounded hills green with grass or brown with wheat and often topped by villages, their white walls and gold-brown roofs brilliant in the evening light; and then into the Sierras themselves, where the slanting sun made deep velvety hollows in the mountainside and clumps of umbrella pine, olive and pink oleander softened the grim edges. All at once we came on the mines of the Rio Tinto, whose angry red cliffs leaped up from the green country around and brooded, sinister, over the little workmen's huts clustered at their foot: it was an inhuman locality with a feel of poison in the air and a sense of remoteness from life, and one passed thankfully from it to the Sierras again, to wide magnificent views in which peak after peak rose and sank like the waves of a troubled sea. The passengers never looked out of the window from start to finish but complained unremittingly of the heat.

Some little way from Aracena is La Peña de Arias Montano, where the famous sanctuary of the Virgen de los Angeles was built. It came into being in the normal way, by the Virgin appearing to a small boy as he minded his goats on the mountainside; and there is something attractive in the idea of this happening in a place named after the consulting theologian to the Council of Trent. There are many of these little shrines all over Spain, faithfully visited by the people of the region, who swear by their own Virgin, of the Rocks, or the Snows, or the Angels or whatever it may be and maintain her superiority over the Virgins of others. To reach it, as so often with places of beauty or interest in Spain, one had either to go on foot as a pilgrim or hire a vehicle, as there was no bus at all. But the taxi-man who drove me to the hotel agreed to make the trip for a reasonable sum and first thing on the following morning he appeared, smiling broadly, wearing his Sunday best and with a flower in his buttonhole.

The little chapel stood on a flat grassy space halfway up the mountain, which rose sharply to a peak behind it. A low stone wall enclosed the space on the outer edge and, sitting on this, I had a glorious view over the Sierras de Aracena with far below the little *pueblo* of Alajar, from which on this Sunday morning arose a steady clapping of tongues and chiming of bells. Inside the chapel the famous Virgin sat in her private house of gold behind the High Altar, beset with artificial flowers and gilt and silver leaves. She was a little painted doll, smaller than usual, with a great dusty tinsel headdress, a long flowing train of shabby brocade and a sweet, insipid face. Near by in the sacristy were hanging all kinds of little possessions brought in thanks for help or favours received: a baby's shoes, children's frocks, a crutch, wax limbs and eyes, a pair of grubby trousers, all the humble offerings of people with almost nothing to spare to pay their debt; and there was a photograph of a young man who had fought with the Blue Division in Russia and had returned, his faith intact—as a caption informed us—after three years in a concentration camp. Chickens ran gaily in and out: somewhere a boy was playing a tune on a pipe. Five old ladies were sitting in the church, fanning themselves and chatting and laughing as if they were drinking tea at home; but in a minute or two a young priest entered with a little flock of pilgrims, at which the naughty old things flung themselves on their knees and began in a penetrating gabble to recite the rosary.

The priest now said Mass for everyone in the sanctuary. His party was spending the day of rest in a typically innocent and charming Spanish way. They had come, fasting, by chara-banc, to hear Mass and take Communion in a famous shrine and afterwards would have their meal on the grass under the trees, with a little singing and picking of wild flowers until it was time to go home again. Very typical too was the composition of the flock: the majority were young girls in white veils and blouses with long sleeves, consciously nubile and given to blushing and giggling: a sprinkling of old women in black, mostly with heavy moustaches, and one or two old men who tried to behave as if they were not really there; and two youths who acted as servers, one thin, anxious and ardent, the other plump, sallow and smug. And there was, of course, one exceed-ingly plain young woman who was more devout than the rest of them put together and whose piercing jay's voice rose high above the others as they chanted.

Meanwhile the taxi-driver had met or made a friend and the pair of them were smoking and drinking and taking life to pieces in the little open-air café. Neither had visited the sanctuary, such things being inappropriate to males in their prime and only to be taken at all seriously when the cold grip of age had sapped their confidence a little. They said if it was all the same to me they should like to remain a little longer, as there was so much to discuss, and I spent a pleasant hour or so lying in the long cool grass, enjoying the country and listening to the sustained grumble of voices that floated up from the little *pueblo* below, far beyond earshot in any land but this. As a reward for patience the taxi-driver took another and longer way home, through mountains covered with sweet chesnut and tall waving fern and gay with wild flowers of blue and yellow (Ford remarks approvingly of this district that it is "quite park-like and English"), while he explained everything over his shoulder; and instead of treating us to the usual blank, animal stare the women along the road smiled in welcome and waved their hands as if grace were on them.

The Hotel Sierpes was nonchalant and friendly in the good Spanish way. Its clock struck twelve when it meant to say one, and often would allow several hours to pass without striking at all. A placard hung on the wall giving notice of mealtimes and bearing no relation to fact whatever. The meals themselves, on the other hand, never varied: I would sometimes observe, with a glutton's gleeful anticipation, baskets of prawns being carried in or fat capons being plucked in the little garden outside the kitchen door, yet all that later appeared on the public table was the unwearying fried cod and the tireless veal cutlet. The proprietor and his wife had a remarkably contented and well-nourished air. A small mystery lurked in the patio where, from the heart of a tangle of red geraniums, there came ever and anon the deep, thrilling notes of a pig: try as I would, I never succeeded in clapping eyes on this solitary animal or discovered his position in the household, and to the end he continued only a voice, plaintive, at times even querulous and yet fundamentally of a sweet resignation.

Luncheon today happened to be at four o'clock and it was after six when, the siesta concluded, I got up and went to see La Gruta de las Maravillas at the lower end of the town. No one else appeared anxious to see it at that hour, and the custodian informed me that the charge for one person alone would be fifty pesetas. It seemed a good deal of money for a grotto, and I was turning away when a tiny motor car bursting with huge Portuguese drove up, and the old lady excitedly told me we could now form a group. This brought the price down to fifteen pesetas each, a sum which struck consternation to the hearts of the Portuguese; but their endeavours to beat it down came to nothing and we all passed inside, in the charge of a scowling, handsome boy.

The caves stretched underground for over a thousand meters and to cover the distance along the narrow twisting corridors and up and down the greasy slopes and slippery ladders took more than an hour. It was a weird and marvelous place: there were row upon row of pale gleaming stalagmites like the pipes of an immense organ, banks of the mineral formation like mighty drifts of snow and little side caves which were encrusted with what looked like starry white flowers, each petal exquisitely chiselled. Now one would come on the startling likeness of a horse's head, or of a lion slinking down a mountain path, or of a statue of Our Lady, of trees, of leaves, of children; and from time to time one would pass an underground lake of a brilliant, horrifying blue, like some Australian liqueur.

It was the first grotto I had seen in my life and I was enchanted; but the Portuguese, who had kept up a surly mutter in their bizarre language the whole way along, suddenly halted in their tracks and declared they should go no farther. They must at once be led again to the light of day. In vain the guide explained that we were about halfway through and might just as well persevere to the end: they merely shook their heads and growled. Back the unfortunate boy had to go, while I sat down in one of the largest caverns to wait. It was tall and gloomy as a Spanish cathedral, full of curious shadowy shapes that seemed to approach and recede like the vaguely threatening figures in a nightmare: strange echoes ran through it and the soft steady fall of drops from the roof into the lake below began as time went on to wear on the nerves. Sitting on a damp boulder in the twilight I hoped that the guide would not forget to return. Forty minutes passed and I was about to give way to panic when he came bounding along, almost too blown to speak, and much ruffled in his demeanour, as if the Portuguese had tried to recover a part of their door-money. I asked what ailed him, and he said that he had run all the way back as he did not like to think of me alone there and perhaps afraid. His kindness and consideration in bolting along those dangerous unlit paths were really touching, the more so as he was an ignorant peasant lad of no manners, given to shouting roughly, "Mind your head! Look out! Come along!": and once when, contrary to the rules, I had touched one of the stalagmites he had given me a sharp, governessy slap on the hand. Now we finished the course very amiably together and at the end of it he would not take the few pesetas I offered him.

I next climbed up to the ruined castle on the hill overlooking the *pueblo*. Here there was another sanctuary, dedicated to Our Lady of Major Sorrows, a full-sized lady dressed in white muslin gown and black velvet cloak, with a rich silver headdress and rhinestone necklace. Her face wore an agonized expression, with glass tears carefully glued on either cheek. Here again were Sunday pilgrims, two flocks of women chattering away like starlings, each under the care of a priest. One of these, with the long sad face of the funny man of a party, was smoking, cracking jokes, scrambling up and down on the ruins and generally emphasizing his humanity. The other, young and handsome, had picked out the three most beautiful girls in his charge and, having posed them against the sanctuary door, was about to take their photograph.

Two young girls of the *pueblo* now attached themselves to me with the simplicity of their kind. They drew my attention to the notable sights of the town spread out below us, the *parroquia*, the hospital run by nuns, the bull-ring (where Litri and Gonzalez had been the week before, they said with enormous pride, kissing their fingers to the air), the *pelota* field and even the pond where the women did their washing. Both were servants, paid about ten shillings a month, they told me, working from eight in the morning until after midnight every day of the year, although how they came to be on the mountainside now they did not explain; and neither had a father, one having died, the other having been killed in the war. At this, the younger of them burst into wild, hopeless giggles. I asked what the joke was, and she replied that it was just to think that her father had died in his bed while the other girl's father had been shot. The sense was a little obscure, the humour a little robust, and on the whole it seemed wise to allow the matter to drop.

Next they pointed to a little church at one end of the town and began to tell me in sinking voices of something that had been done in front of it, something fearful and only to be recounted with bated breath; but they broke off abruptly as a fat middle-aged man came toiling round a bend of the steep hill with a bucket of water in either hand, groaning with heat and fatigue. It was the keeper of the monument, who every morning and evening had to climb up and water the few young trees that had been planted by order of the local authority. A fine comic entrance he made too, sweating and moaning and cursing, his body swaying with every step and his legs on the verge of buckling beneath him.

"All for twenty pesetas a day," he complained. Ay! Spain was a bad country, where no one could earn anything. Come a good winter gale, he added with gloomy delight, and the trees would be blown down and his sweat wasted. He tossed the water fretfully about their roots and turned to go, but suddenly bethought him of something else: when the next war started, he observed, they would drop one of those new bombs on the *pueblo* and that would be that. The prospect seemed to revive him a little, and he sat down on the rampart with us with an almost contented look on his face.

"Do you smoke?" he inquired. "I thought so. If by chance you could spare one . . . *muchisimas gracias*. In Spain, only prostitutes smoke. And of course rich women in Madrid. If an ordinary girl of the people were to smoke, the people would talk about it and she would never get a husband. But you French have different ideas.

"Where is your husband?" he then asked, in a sudden worry. *No husband.* Ay, ay, ay. As if one thing led to another, he pointed out a rock overhanging the cliff which, he said, was very handy for suicides. A man threw himself off it last winter, and he enacted the poor fellow's last moments with enormous gusto while the two little girls shrieked with pleasure. By now he was as gay as a cricket.

"*Bueno,*" he said at last, with a beaming smile. "Soon we shall all be blown to atoms."

I left the three of them shouting and laughing over the agreeable fate in store, and walked down the hill again, through the *pueblo* to the little church the maids had been discussing before the keeper arrived. It was quite shut up and falling into ruins: the windows were broken and hens ran to and fro over the weedy desolation of the yard. An old woman came out of a house near by and stared curiously at me.

"*Está siempre cerrada* (Is it always shut)?" I called to her and she slowly nodded her head.

"*Cerrada por siempre!*"

The little alteration of phrase and her manner of speaking suggested that further inquiry would not be welcome. In her voice I seemed to catch an echo of the pain left behind by the war, the bitterness of life that had to be lived out among its memories. She turned and with hesitating step walked back into her house, slamming the door. What was it that happened here, visible from her little windows, that even today could only be murmured?

After dinner that evening in the plaza the Sunday evening celebrations were in full swing under the illumined trees. A brass band was playing Spanish tunes at the upper end of it, and although it was past midnight the place swarmed with tiny children shrieking at the tops of their lungs, seemingly inexhaustible. The two little servants hailed me as an old and precious friend but refused, with consternation, to join in a drink at the café. A number of little girls were dancing very gravely and prettily to the music when all at once they were set upon by a gang of small boys, whose leader, aged about eleven, was puffing at a cigarette: at which they were suddenly transformed into demons and a frenzied brawl took place in which no method was barred and the boys had much the worst of it. At last I went home to bed: it seemed that everyone in Aracena had a radio, every radio was on at full strength and that every door and window was open, as if a determined communal effort were being made to drown some other faint, persistent voice that no one wished to hear. The shindy went on until well into the dawn; I tossed and turned while every now and again the pig that lurked behind the geraniums would groan as if in sympathy.

9

ARACENA WAS SO DELIGHTFUL a place, the next hop of my journey so fraught with the uncertainty of anything but discomfort, that perhaps it was by unconscious design I overslept and missed the only bus of the day to Repilado. The young host was much amused to see me reappear: he had spent a long while on the night before working out a plan of travel across country to Jerez de los Caballeros, urging me at the same time to go right back to Seville and start from there. Now, wearing the purple blouse and yellow cord in fidelity to some religious vow, he played by the hour with his baby son in the parlour. Each unsteady step the infant took, every foolish sound that fell from his lips, caused the father's face to light up with a love and pride that were splendid to see. The wife meanwhile was sewing away close at hand, with the serene, indulgent look that Spanish mothers have at such times.

A whole day of glorious idleness stretched ahead: or so I believed. But as I strolled by the public washing-place on the way to the cemetery, all the women there began to scream like magpies. By some mysterious law of nature women washing clothes in the open air are always at their most redoubtable: it seems to arouse the fiend in them; and these were no exception to it.

"*Hola!* look at the foreigner!"

"Look at the Frenchie!"

"*Fea! Fea! Fea!* (Ugly!)"

"She is not like us! She doesn't work! She doesn't wash!"

"She *cannot* wash!"

The last sally was altogether too much and, climbing the low wall that encircled the water troughs, I declared my intention of washing. The younger women shrieked with laughter as if nothing so absurd had come their way before, but an old lady made room for me beside her and told me not to mind them. She explained how washing was done in Aracena. You soaked and soaped the garment and rubbed it vigorously up and down on a slab of ridged marble until the dirt was out: then you rinsed it, soaped it again and spread it in the sun: and when it was dry you washed it all over again. By these back-breaking methods the clothes dropped on the hotel floor in the morning return so dazzling white before dinner, at a cost of a few pesetas. After an hour or so my spine was in such a way I hardly expected ever to walk upright again: but, in dread of their tongues, I soaped and rubbed and rinsed in quiet desperation, inwardly thanking God I hadn't to do it every day.

But gradually the atmosphere began to change. The mysterious truculence of the Woman Washing gave way to the innate trade-unionism, equally mysterious, of the Female. Down at the end of the line I could hear someone telling her neighbour that I was an English writer, staying at the Sierpes, that I had visited the Virgen de la Peña in Romero's taxi, had bought ice-creams in the *plaza* for Rosalita Moreno and Maria Gomez, and that I was about to cross Extremadura alone: the local grapevine was up to standard. The information was passed all round, gone into, exclaimed over: the giggles and wisecracks came to an end: I was in. There remained only the eternal Spanish question of where my husband was. Even the Gypsy, whose bold, vivid, saucy face marked her out from all those other vivid faces and who yesterday had tagged after me through the town cursing and shrieking for money, now grew sweet as a dove and volunteered to sing if I would. After the usual discussion of who should be first, she broke into a melancholy snatch of *flamenco* and danced a little at the end of it. I followed with "The Lark in the Pure Air," rendered in a small cracked voice and with frequent interruptions where I forgot the words. It was received with polite enthusiasm and declared to be *muy fino*. And now the sun was high in the heavens and, as the *practicante* was to see me directly after luncheon, I had to say good-bye; and they parted from me with great kindness and good will, all resentment forgotten.

The midday meal was enlivened by a huge excitable family of Portuguese. From their clothes and jewels they seemed to have plenty of money, unless indeed they had put it all on their backs: but they found the modest charge of thirty pesetas a head for lunch too steep and they were resolved on getting it down to twenty-five. First they claimed a reduction on account of their numbers, but the argument fell on deaf ears and they went on to complicated proposals concerning the menu. If they went without bread and wine? If they skipped the egg dish? Well, then, if they took two portions of meat only and shared it out among the lot of them? Or could the fruit be suppressed? The chatter went on and on in a crescendo of parsimony until at last it was borne in on them that they would not succeed and they composed themselves to munch their way through the list in gloomy silence.

I ate very little, being weary of the too familiar procession and not knowing how often in the days to come I should look hungrily back to it. Presently the landlord came in to say the *practicante* was waiting outside. "But there is no hurry at all," he added with an expansive wave of the arm. "Please take your time!" The practicante is an admirable Spanish institution, something less than a doctor and more than a male nurse, who renders all kinds of small medical services for practically nothing at all. Some of them are medical students who are helping to keep themselves in this way, others have never managed to pass the examinations: this latter class produces some rich Dickensian figures, capital entertainers nearly all. The one today was young and handsome and very smartly dressed: too smartly dressed really, for a man who was about to give an injection for less than a shilling. He had set up a bath of spirit over a lamp and was stewing a needle in it as if to prepare for a major operation; and he examined the phial I gave him with knitted brows and compressed lips, as if life itself hung in the balance. While he waited for the needle to stew, he fell into conversation and it soon emerged that here was one more passionate follower of the ring. Litri! He had been at school with him: a great man, a man of few words. He took out his wallet and produced a photograph, faded and lovingly thumbed, of the pair of them together.

"Some people say it is dying out," I remarked.

"Ha! Never, never, never, never!" He snatched his needle up and planted it in my arm with the furious precision of a *banderillero*. "Never!" he said again, grimly swabbing. We sat on awhile with my aching arm between us and he gave me a lot of interesting information about the finances of the ring, the cost of bulls, the prize-money of fighters, the cuts taken by hangers-on, the expense of keeping the Press in a suitable state of mind. Only as he got up to go did a professional thought suddenly occur to him.

"But why do you have these injections?" he asked with a little frown. "You are not afraid of our water? It is the best in the world."

"I know: but I am going on to Portugal."

The falsity of this I think he instantly perceived, but it mollified him none the less, as honey-lies so often will; and he bowed with infinite grace over the five-peseta note I handed him.

After the siesta I walked for hours about the countryside, as beautiful as any in the world: indeed, Aracena is a place where you could dream your life away. The silvery grey of the olive against the pale gold of the scorched earth and fading grass was very lovely, as were the leaves of the eucalyptus shivering daintily in the still gold light of evening. Little rosy twists of cloud drifted about in a vast green sky. A flock of sheep came ambling over the side of a hill, driven by two old men and two clever young dogs, all of them, men and beasts, turned to gold by the last of the sun; and as they went the hundreds of sheep-bells rang with the strange note that rings in the heart of a waterfall, sad, monotonous and dead. Time seemed in a curious way to be standing still: I felt as if I had been there many times before and seen that very flock moving along in just that drowsy manner: or that, returning years hence, I should find them all again.

This last evening in Aracena left behind an impression of great beauty and peace: the impression left by the night that followed was equally sharp, no less typical, but devoid of all charm. Extraordinary thumpings and sawings, never explained, continued into the early hours while from the heart of his geranium lair the pig fretfully stirred and moaned; and at about half past four somebody came and thundered on the front door of the hotel, bawling, "*Señor! Señor! SEÑOR!!*" as if himself and the man he wanted were the only two people on earth. To say that Spaniards are lacking in consideration for others is not enough: they do not really believe that others exist; and yet there is a pure, intense quality about their egoism that makes it admirable and attractive.

This time I caught the rickety little bus to Repilado, which was already crammed with passengers by the time I got to it. The two best seats were occupied by members of the Guardia Civil, who had swathed their shiny black hats with green canvas to protect them from dust, much as furniture might be swathed against the coming of the sweep. Leaning on their rifles and looking straight ahead, they spoke to none but each other and then only briefly and sternly, in the accents of another country. The rest of the people shouted gaily to each other throughout the ride, which was a beautiful one through mile after mile of chestnut-wooded hills.

At Repilado, of course, the daily bus to Fregenal had left and there was nothing for it but a local train, something to avoid whenever possible. With hundreds of squatting figures I waited on the roasting platform for an hour or two until it came limping and coughing up and we all made a determined rush for places. Then it moved gently off up the line with a very singular motion indeed, in which the leap of a frog, the bounce of a pogo-stick and the canter of a very short fat pony all were brought to mind. The windows were wide open, impossible indeed to close, so that when it passed through one of the many tunnels we got the full richness of the brown, stinking smoke. There was only one other person in my compartment, a youth who sang *flamenco* every inch of the way, often the same little phrase over and over and over again, with a fixed gloom of countenance. But as we drew level with the engine of another train in the station of Cumbres Mayores, the driver of it hung out of his cage and lustily sang back to him, his light blue eyes rolling in his sooty face: this cheered my companion wonderfully and the pair sang *à deux* with great spirit and pleasure until the trains moved on and dragged them apart.

At Fregenal, again, I learned that the bus to Jerez de los Caballeros had left at 6:30 that morning; but the porter who seized my bags at the station undertook to lead me to a most delightful inn, and only a mile or so away. Looking at the dreary, featureless waste that was Fregenal de la Sierra as it danced in the heat, I was seized with a kind of despair. The resources of the entire place could hardly take up more than a quarter hour; and I meditated on the lunacy of travellers who strike out on adventurous paths of their own, forgetting that if places are neglected by others there is very likely a sound reason for it. But if the material resources of Fregenal were poor, the human ones—as so often in Spain—were considerable. The *mozo* paused at a crossroads, where a little group of men were standing round a gasoline pump, to ask which *fonda* would be best for me; and they naturally wanted to know in turn why anyone should stay in Fregenal at all. Then they said that a truck would shortly pass through the *pueblo* on its way to Jerez de los Caballeros and they should put me on it. They fetched a wooden chair and sat me down in the shade of the pump while the *mozo*, refusing to be paid off, stretched himself on the ground beside with the air of a man whose time is his own. After an hour or two a cloud of dust on the horizon announced the approach of the truck; but the driver did not at first take to the suggestion at all. The kind of long Spanish debate followed in which all parties appear to be furiously angry. But all at once he turned to me with a broad grin and a cry of "*Vamos! Vamos!*" as if it were I who capriciously was holding things up. The bags were hoisted to the pinnacle of the oil drums stowed in the rear and carefully made fast with ropes; and, wedged between the driver and his mate in the sweltering cabin, I was borne rapidly off towards my goal.

The distance was covered in something over an hour; and but for the happy chance of the truck passing through I should not only have kicked my heels for the rest of that day in Fregenal but spent a good part of the next morning in the bus as it trotted from one village to the next gathering the people up. In rural Spain, at least, it is far better to arrive than to travel, however hopefully.

The name of the best hotel in Jerez de los Caballeros was El Brillante: a name which by sheer stupendous unsuitability has burned itself on my mind forever. A heavy young woman lounged against the post of the front door, languidly hitting at flies with a fan. She made no reply when I asked for a room but slowly looked me up and down with suspicion and a kind of animal resentment. At last she turned on her heel and walked into a little den, where a whispered colloquy, plainly audible to me, took place: was I to be admitted or not? She is alone, you say? Quite alone. And how did she come? Off a truck: Pedro saw her and carried her luggage. And what does she want here? Who knows? Hm. . . . And alone! Quite alone. *Bueno*. . . . The young woman came back and reluctantly said I could have a room. There were two lumpy beds in it, both unmade, one small enamel washbasin perched on an iron stand and any number of chamber-pots. I asked for a jug of water and she stared at me as if out of all patience with the whims of foreigners. While she set off at a snail's pace to see if water could be allowed, I made for the lavatory and tentatively opened the door, only to reel back at once in dismay. But there was nothing for it; and, tying a handkerchief round my face like a bandit, I plunged bravely into the interior.

Having washed and changed and brushed a little of the grit out of my hair, I went down to the dining-room. Now the young woman greeted me with the ghost of a smile: the shock of my appearance was dying away, the hardship of having to look at me was sturdily being faced and her natural good manners were reasserting themselves. With an air of subdued triumph she placed on the table a mound of cold runner beans and potatoes which had apparently been sprayed with scented brilliantine. It was followed by an omelet lying in a pool of dark green oil and then by a piece of grey meat of so pungent and horrible an aroma that all at once the room began to go round and round and I could only feebly gesture for it to be taken away. Three sour male figs completed the grisly banquet: at such times the wedge of half-baked bread and half-liter of local rotgut wine appear rather in the guise of delicacies.

Yet I was not sorry to have come. Jerez de los Caballeros is an enchanting little town built by the Knights Templar in the thirteenth century, with narrow, twisting streets of white-washed houses, each fronted by its boxes of pink and red geraniums, or flanked by lemon and orange trees, and all so clean and gay as to have the air of perpetual *fiesta*. These narrow lanes struggle up to the top of a fairly steep hill on which stands the principal church of Santa Maria and from which there is a fine view of the Sierras rising all round; for Jerez lies in a dip of the plain like a saucer. On another, lower hill some five minutes' walk away is San Bartolomeo, the lacy red tower inlaid with bright blue tiles, and somewhat lower again San Miguel: three splendid churches in the one small place and seeming as usual, with all the gold-leaf, the pictures, statues, the heavily encrusted ornamentation of the high altars, rather too grand for it. All are shut when not in actual use but a foreigner need only stand and look at the door for someone to appear as if by magic, waving a key. Here again in every tower were the nesting storks: one stood, white against the deep blue sky, on the very summit of the image of Our Lady over Santa Maria, hundreds of feet above the *pueblo*, apparently lost in reflection. Their habit of building on church belfries, Ford says, is held out by the priests to the people as a good example in the selection of abodes; but, he adds, with the characteristic Ford chuckle, "*Detras de la cruz está el diabolo.*"

Time passed very pleasantly in wandering about and night was beginning to fall when, with sinking heart, I returned to El Brillante. The fat young woman was on guard at the door with her fan. Did her whole life perhaps go by in looking up and down that street and aiming those half-hearted blows at the flies? And the creature always missed, invariably she missed them. There were no safer flies in the whole of Spain. And no young woman in Spain had a sadder, duller, heavier face. Had she abandoned hope of whatever it was she looked up and down the street to find? She was perfectly reconciled now to me and flashed a smile of welcome with the ominous news that dinner was on the table. I passed inside to confront it, leaving her to the contemplation of destiny.

10

AFTER LESS than forty-eight hours off the beaten track I was aching to be on it again. The bus for Zafra left at eight in the morning and, as it is impossible for anyone in a small provincial hotel to rise before nine at the earliest, I had been given an alarm clock whose fierce ticking hour after hour through the night had greatly contributed to my unhappiness. The *mozo* who had sworn to be at the doors of the hotel at 7:30 had not appeared by a quarter to eight and I had therefore to run through the streets in search of another; and by the time I had fished one up, drowsy with *aguardiente* in one of the seedier bars, the first had arrived after all and the second, after some discussion, had to be paid off. It was nearly ten past eight when we reached the square and there was no sign of any bus. My flesh crept at the sight of the empty place, for there is never more than one bus a day in such parts and two further meals at El Brillante would certainly be the end of me. But a woman selling *churros* near the stop declared that it had not yet come and could not be expected for a little time yet: that anyone should have supposed it would leave at the proper hour seemed to entertain her very much.

This kind woman gave me her chair to sit on while she went on with her frying. For equipment all she had was a round tin with a twig fire inside, a round pan on the top of it full of sizzling oil, a basin of dough and something oddly like a seventeenth-century clyster. With this she squeezed ropes of dough into the oil and poked them to and fro with two long iron pins until they were crisp and brown and as digestible as lead piping; then she drew them out and snipped them with scissors into lengths according to the appetite of the customer, charging a penny or so for every six inches. Countrymen and women better acquainted than I with the behaviour pattern of the local bus were slowly now assembling with their chickens and vegetables and babies and stood round the brazier munching foot after foot of the delicacy with a fixed gravity of demeanour. I watched them, fascinated and appalled as ever by Spanish endurance; and thinking in her goodness that I was hungry the woman cut me seventeen inches or so as a free gift and stood over me, maternally smiling, until I had eaten it up. When at last the bus rumbled into the square I rose to meet it with a sense of having swallowed a bagful of marbles.

The bus stood out as a strange vehicle in a land where vehicles are apt to be strange. It was so old and weary that it seemed impossible it should last the day; and such was the lack of coordination between the body and the nose that passengers often seemed to be travelling a course different from that steered by the driver. Yet the class distinction was kept up, the first in front being stuffed with fat men and smelling strongly of *anis*, with which they had fortified themselves before leaving, and the second behind given up to the less prosperous and their own appropriate odours. The road it went was so pitted and scarred and furrowed that the driver's whole attention was given up to tacking about to this side and that in the effort to avoid the worst of the ravines, and he remained deaf to the minatory hooting of faster vehicles behind who wished to overtake him: until one of these in exasperation butted us savagely in the rear, after which a lookout man was appointed on the back seat to raise a cry of *Coche! Coche!*

whenever there was need; and this in turn would be taken up and chorused by us all until at last it penetrated even the driver's consciousness and he would pull sulkily to one side, when the overtaker sped by enveloping us in a thick cloud of dust.

At every stop fat men got out and more fat men came piling in. My neighbour, whose sixteen stone of baking flesh had served me as a giant and unnecessary hot-water bottle, actually got out and in again because he had lost a piece of money. He then gave a demonstration of the very Spanish state of mind in which the person is magnificently unaware of the existence of anyone or anything outside himself. First he searched the floor under his own seat and not finding the money there thought it must have rolled under mine. Down he went on hands and knees to look, pushing my legs to and fro as if I had been a piece of furniture, muttering to himself the while and impatiently tugging at my skirt when it got in his line of vision. All was to no purpose and he was already despondently making for the door when a new idea struck him: he returned and, taking me in his arms, lifted me up without a word and peered at the empty seat for a moment or two: then, exclaiming and shaking his head, he dropped me again with the same entire simplicity and got out once more, this time for good.

When the end of the terrible journey was reached my clothes were coated with dust and my head felt as if it were about to explode, while every bone in my body ached with its own separate ache. But the experience had not been wholly bad because once again I had been able to admire the patience and good humour of Spanish people in circumstances that would start most of us writing furiously to Members of Parliament.

The small city of Zafra lies in a plain, a great parched basin of snuff-coloured earth with only a few huge boulders of rock leaping up here and there to break the monotony. It is an ancient city, known to history long before the time of the Romans, but there is little now to see of interest. The buildings are mediocre and down-at-heel, sadly in need of paint and repair, and the gardens wear a jaded, wilting look as if the surrounding decay had discouraged even them. But today was the feast of St. Peter and there was great animation in the shabby streets. A horse fair with dealers from all over the region was in progress at the moment and in the evening there was to be that most bizarre of Spanish conceptions, a comic bull-fight.

The fair was held on open ground at the edge of the city and was as wild a scene as anyone could have hoped for. Horses and donkeys and mules of every colour and age and disposition stretched away as far as the eye could see, crowded together in the shade of what trees there were or sweating and twitching under the wicked sun. Here would be a pitiful nag so old and weary it seemed impossible it had ever made its way to the market: there, a fiery young stallion lashing out with his heels at any beast or man that came within range. A deafening clamour filled the air as the owners vociferously argued their points to customers, who skeptically rubbed their chins and shook their heads. With wonderful skill men threaded their way through the surging crowds on the backs of mules, riding without bit or saddle, perched well back on the rump and guiding the animal with a single rope attached to the noseband and held in the left hand. These creatures move with a gait of their own, very curious to see, faster than a trot but without any jogging or jolting: a quick, smooth, dainty, almost a mincing, walk. Some of the riders were small children who showed the same ease and adroitness and courage as the men.

A Gypsy shouted to me to come over and look at his horse, a young animal of a warm chestnut colour with a fine head. I did so, and was unwise enough to inquire the price of it. Nobody in Spain is ever interested in information for its own sake and the Gypsy assumed that I wanted to buy the horse —indeed, nothing would convince him of the contrary. He pulled its mouth open to display the strong young teeth, he drew attention to the splendid muscles, he leaped upon its back and showed its paces: he undertook to deliver it to my hotel.

"There never was such a bargain!" he yelled, seizing me by the arm and shaking me.

By now we were ringed by interested spectators, each eagerly trying to get his word in.

"I cannot take the horse to London," I explained.

"Why not? Why not? It is just the thing for London."

"The Customs would not like it."

"Customs!" said the Gypsy, and spat.

A little gnome of a man with the beard of several days on his chin and a gentle, falsetto voice intervened at this point.

"The *Señora* does not want to buy your horse," he fluted. "I know what the *Señora* wants."

"Leave my customer alone," the Gypsy roared, turning on him.

"She does not want to buy your horse."

"She asked the price. Of course she does. Woman! You will buy my horse? You will never get this chance again."

There was a growl of agreement from the lookers-on. The sense of the meeting appeared to be that having come this far I ought to clinch the deal like an honest woman and not waste any more time. In another minute the horse would have been mine, together with a superb opportunity for testing the statements of Borrow and Ford on the hazards of riding in Spain. I laughed nervously and waved my hand and hurried away, with the Gypsy staring after me in surprise and indignation. Presently with a pattering of feet the little gnome came smiling up and slipped his arm into mine.

"I knew it," he said. "Come with me and I will show you something lovely."

"Where?"

"Just over there. Just on the other side of the little hill. *Una cosa bonita.* Come."

We strolled towards the little hill, the gnome trotting at my side and explaining as he went that he was a widower, that his wife had died the year before, that nevertheless he still was young at heart and that above all he thoroughly understood women. But when we reached the brow of the hill there was nothing whatever to be seen on the other side but the great undulating spaces of hot, snuff-coloured earth.

"Where is this *cosa bonita* of yours?"

"Listen," said the gnome, in a cosy sort of way. "If you like me, we could go together."

"What?!"

"If you like me," he said patiently.

I burst out laughing and turned back towards the fair at a smart pace with the gnome hopping and skipping along behind.

"Why not, *Señora?* I am not perhaps young," he piped, "but will you find a better? And can you be sure you won't like me, unless you try?"

"Excuse me."

"Excuse *me*," he then said very politely, and held his peace.

Our reappearance after so short an interval aroused a good deal of amusement.

"No luck?" shouted one of the dealers.

"What did I tell you?" thundered the Gypsy. "She wanted my horse."

The gnome shrugged his shoulders right up to his ears and let them fall again. A woman who came alone by herself to the fair and talked to the men freely and shamelessly, as loose women do; and then turned the first offer down without so much as inquiring into the details of it! It was beyond him altogether.

"*Es loca!*" he told the Gypsy, placing a significant finger to his temple. "You are well out of it."

Some of the richer dealers or those who had done a good business appeared at luncheon in the Hotel Cabaña, where their swarthy faces, black linen smocks and emphatic style of eating marked them out from the rest of the clientele. The meal the Cabaña served was immense, even by Spanish standards: heaped plates of cold fish and salad were followed by a vast *puchero* or meat stew which also apparently was a mere appetizer, as after it came slabs of veal fried in batter. In Spain, land of extremes, you eat too much or not at all. Undismayed by the temperature of the dining-room, which was roughly that of a moderate oven, the guests did marvelous work, munching their way steadily through the mountains in front of them and using the blade of the knife as a spoon to secure every last crumb. My breakfast still weighed upon me, and I took nothing but bread and a little wine and waited for the dessert. This consisted of a green banana and four tiny green pears. I asked the waiter for an orange, but he said that unfortunately they had all gone. It seemed to distress him, for a few seconds later the proprietor himself came up to inform me that oranges at this time of year were not worth eating. So, leaving the banana and the pears, I went out to the market round the corner and bought some oranges for myself. The proprietor saw me carrying them in and regretfully shook his head.

"They are no good, those oranges, I'm afraid," he remarked.

They were delicious, of course, but no matter: he had saved his face and preserved the forms.

A hush fell on the town as the stifling hours of the afternoon went slowly by: it is the only period of the Spanish day when there is something a little like peace. Presently the citizens rose from their beds and streamed down to the bull-ring to see the *corrida bufa*. It was the first spectacle of the kind ever to come my way and I was curious to see how the performers would go about it, for bull-fighting seemed as unpromising a subject for comedy as murder itself. Before the chief turn came on, however, we had to sit through three "straight" *corridas* of the miserable type commonly seen in small provincial rings. The matadors wore ordinary Andalusian dress with tight trousers and sash, being unable to afford the glittering *traje de luces:* likewise they had no money for real bulls and this was as well, since they possessed neither courage nor skill to fight them. The creatures that came out one by one to be slowly and incompetently butchered were ugly and emaciated, with the appearance of starving cows: the second was so wild and fast that it was an embarrassingly long time before the men dared leave their shelters to engage it, and the third was resolved not to fight at all, but careered round and round the arena looking desperately for a place where he might be quiet and safe. The audience laughed so much at both of these that for a moment it seemed as if the *bufa* had begun after all.

After an interval the gates opened again and five little dwarfs tripped gravely into the ring. They were dressed in farcical clothes, the father in a bowler hat and cutaway coat, the mother in a red velvet *robe de style* with a long trailing skirt, a nurse-maid with frilly drawers showing beneath her apron and a baby, wheeled in a chair and sucking a bottle. This grotesque little party arranged itself as a family group in the middle of the arena, while the fifth, got up as a photographer, importantly set his camera in front of them and buried his head in the folds of a black cloth. They held the tableau in perfect immobility for several minutes: not knowing what to expect, I could not imagine what they were doing and began to grow restive: they were a funny sight, but surely not as funny as all that. But meanwhile there was a steadily growing murmur of excitement from the crowd. Suddenly the gates opened once more and a bull came tearing in, to the rear of the photographer and in line with his backside, so temptingly offered. Not one of the little people so much as stirred: the mother and father continued to grin at the camera in the fatuous elation of parenthood, the baby sucked his bottle, the nursemaid leered, the photographer went on taking his sights with his diminutive hand on the bulb. The bull paused in astonishment, bellowed, pawed the ground and charged the photographer. With the thunder of flying hooves in his ears the game little fellow never flinched or moved; and in the next moment a vicious jab of the horn sprawled him headlong in the sand while the family group broke up with every expression of surprise and annoyance.

Wild laughter broke from every part of the audience, in which it was impossible not to join. As well as their passion for bull-fighting, the Spaniards have a mania for being photographed, and that the little dwarfs were so absorbed in this as not to notice the approach of what, in the ordinary way, must have interested them even more, was a deliciously comic idea. Now they sturdily prepared to deal with their new situation. Leaving the baby alone in his chair with the bull snorting and fuming round it, the nursemaid took the *banderillos* and, rudely aping the mannerisms of various celebrated *toreros*, cited the bull with much leaping up and down and display of frilly underpants. As he charged, she ran lightly to meet him with the darts poised above her head, but missed her footing and sat heavily down in front of his nose, the darts still at the ready and a wonderfully foolish look on her face as she stared uneasily up at him. The bull contented himself with trampling her underfoot as he dashed on to attack the father and mother, now arguing fiercely as to which of them should give the *suerte*, snatching the sword from each other's hands, slapping each other's face and paying no heed at all to the bull, who by this time was nearly frantic with rage and impatience. He rolled in the dust, he banged them with the horn, he kicked them and ran them over, but they simply got up again, dusted themselves and without a glance in his direction continued the argument. At last the mother gained her point and, taking the sword and cloak, she rustled over the sand in her clinging velvet to where the bull was standing; but then, only two or three feet away, she turned her back on him and, in exquisite, unforgettable parody of the great *espadas* in their moment of triumph and supremacy, that moment when they have so tamed and dominated the bull that he will stand there quietly until they choose to continue, she sank on one knee and opened her arms to the crowd. She received the customary ovation, as was her right: the drawback was, of course, that she had failed to *mandar* the bull. Bang! To the enormous delight of everyone he sent her flying; but she got up immediately and, having carefully set her dress to rights and adjusted her wig, accomplished the *faena*, caricaturing every move and every pass with lunatic genius until at last, the sword poised steadily in her tiny hand, she struggled forward, kicking her skirts out of the way, to meet the ultimate furious charge and one saw, in sudden horror and with the tears of merriment still wet on the face, that the bull was staggering to and fro in the agony of death.

The *fiesta* went smoothly on through the evening and the night with the hideous uproar essential to its proper enjoyment. Sleep was impossible; and as I tossed and turned in the roasting cupboard that was my room I thought again and again of the brilliant little freaks, the weird, painted faces too large for the crooked bodies, the extremes of valour and gaiety and, underlying it all, the sense of a fearful desperation as they exposed and offered their affliction to the pitiless laughter of the crowd. *Cosas de España!* The dreadful journey into this wilderness had been worth the making.

11

AS A DROWNING MAN comes up for air, at Mérida I sent economy to the devil and stayed at the *parador*. It was a charming house, solid, washed white, with ancient coats of arms above the door and storks nesting in the turrets on the roof: once it had been a Franciscan monastery. In the patio were the remains of Roman columns and an old stone well with creaking chain and bucket, and the bedrooms were small, bare and clean as the cell of a monk. The dining-room was furnished in a simple countrified way and on the walls were old prints of Spanish scenes, such as boar-hunting or a carousal in a wine-cellar, and down the halls and corridors hung ancient maps of a splendid inaccuracy. The meals were delicious, if gargantuan, and they were served by pretty girls in black dresses; and the whole place had the easy-going friendly air of all good Spanish hotels, as if to squeeze money from the visitor were not the end and aim of life. But the keenest pleasure of all was to stand in a snowy bathrobe and watch real hot water pouring into an actual bath: I had forgotten a little what it looked like.

Nearly all the guests were wealthy French people, hurriedly "doing" the Roman remains before they passed on to the more notable cities of the south. They flashed along the highways in their beautiful motor cars from one *parador* to the next, and one could imagine what they had to say about the inns of Spain when they got back to Paris or Lyons. Remarkably good, but remarkably! Who says that in Spain one is uncomfortable? *Trop cher, évidemment;* but for the rest, *comme de chez-soi!* I should have liked to introduce them to El Brillante.

Of the many splendours of classical Mérida, the theatre is the finest and best preserved today. It is well placed in the dip of a hill a short way from the town, and there are beautiful views from it, of rising and falling plains to one side, of the curiously abrupt peaks of the Sierras de San Servan on the other. To reach it you climb a narrow lane passing the barracks of the Policia Armada, those men in the grey and red uniform who are best given a wide berth; and indeed this morning from behind one of the barred cell-windows a voice was harshly, insistently shouting. In the theatre itself all was peace. A toll-house was at the entrance to collect up the entrance fees, but the gate stood hospitably open and no keeper appeared. Barrows and pickaxes lay about on the ruins, as some kind of restoration was under way, but the workmen were not to be seen. A number of headless figures lolled against the broken columns, eerie in the naturalness and perfection of their limbs and draperies. The lizards and I had the place to ourselves. A week before the Lope de Vega Company from Madrid had given Shakespeare's *Julius Caesar* on this stage, presumably at night, for the sun makes a furnace of it at any other time with the theatregoers of Mérida seated on the grim stone ledges that fan outwards and upwards from it. Spanish endurance must be nearly as great as the Romans' own.

There was a Roman bridge as well, spanning the River Guadiana, much restored but with the robust round arches still intact and with a large bay let in the center of each side where, after dark, the loving couples of the city come and spoon. The river must be very wide when full but now in high summer it had shrunk to two little arms, both of a heavenly blue from the sky's reflection and encircling the raised stony bed in the middle. A few sheep stood at the edge, admiring themselves in the mirroring water, with eight or nine storks in conclave near at hand. An endless stream of loaded donkeys and cows poured over the massive but narrow bridge, and across the river was a long line of rickety hovels where the people lived, and one or two imposing factories where they worked.

A man hailed me as I sat dreaming on the bank and came over at a brisk, threatening pace. He wore a battered felt hat, pink shirt, blue trousers and white sneakers, with a couple of days' black beard on his chin, and he was very cross. He was one of the crossest men I ever met. "This is a bad country. Why do you come?" was the opening gambit he hurled at me before he had properly sat down. All hard work and no money and you couldn't get a passport to go away. You might reach Portugal, perhaps, but things were no better there. And the Government, God, the Government! Schemes for this and that, but it was simply there to protect the rich and everything else was bunk. In England, now, a man got real wages. That was a country to live in! I tried to comfort him by saying that the cost of living was a great deal higher, but he fairly exploded at this. Who cared what the cost of living was? You could pay for it with money. In Spain you couldn't eat. A soldier's pay was fifty centesimos a day. And just try driving a truck for a livelihood, if you want to know what misery is. He sat with me for about twenty minutes scowling and grumbling and then made off as unexpectedly as he had come, at the same lumbering trot; and presently as I too strolled back in the direction of the city he hailed me from the doorway of a rowdy little wineshop next to the bridge and, now wreathed in smiles, attempted to lure me inside.

The next cultural treat was a visit to the ruins of the aqueduct, from which the way led back through the public gardens and here was a monument to St. Eulalia, not the important Spanish saint of that name, but a local martyr born in 292. Although shown in the effigy as an adult lady of forbidding countenance, she had been put to death while still a child: they baked the poor little thing in an oven. From Heaven she continued to watch over the city and acquired a military reputation. A chapel was raised to her on the scene of the crime in 1612, but has vanished long since: indeed, it is remarkable how few evidences are left of Mérida's long and brilliant history. Her flowering under the Romans persisted to the fourth century: in the seventh the Goths raised her to the glory of a metropolitan See, in which she remained until 1120, when it passed to Santiago: the Moors held her from 715 to 1229, using the people with kindness and toleration and, as ever, bringing life and prosperity with them. Yet, apart from the Roman antiquities, there is little to give the sense of a past so rich. Mérida was, of course, occupied by the French and ruthlessly despoiled by them, like the greater part of this region. Describing how even the olive trees on which the peasants depended were cut down by these wretches, Ford grimly remarks: "Among those who most desolated Mérida was General Reynier, a collector of antiquities. The accumulated rubbish in the great courtyard of the conventual shows his handywork." They passed over it like a veritable plague of locusts, and still it may be wondered if they alone were to blame. As a people the Spaniards are curiously indifferent to their past, it may be because so much of it was shaped for them by outsiders: they always ignore what affects their pride. The local tourist officials produce their ecstatic leaflets and nearly every town of any size at all will have its *cronista*, a singlehearted enthusiast who spends his time not merely delving into the past, but tabling for posterity the events of the day, no matter how trival. But if you ask the people you fall in with for information, the usual reply is a shrug. They will assert as a matter of faith that their town is the finest and most interesting in all the Spains, but rarely descend to particulars. And nowhere have I found this characteristic apathy greater than in Mérida, today no longer quite so "poor and almost depopulated" as in the time of Ford, but comfortably asleep, its thoughts reaching no further than the goings-on of the neighbours or the price of pigs.

This opinion was confirmed by two delightful characters I had the luck to encounter, who discussed the local shortcomings with the frankness of men coming from Madrid and Vigo respectively. The first held an important position in the Matadero factory for sausages, ham and tinned meat, of which I had been given many glowing reports, some going so far as to describe it as "absolutely the last word, like Chicago." This proved on examination to have been a little extravagant, but the factory was very clean and appeared to be well run. Every part of the animal was used in some way or another, and my friend showed me a compound made from blood, costing £250 a pound, for use against stomach ulcers. At the present time they were slack and only employing six hundred hands, but in the winter, running to capacity, the number is about twice that. Skilled men earned up to fifty pesetas a day, unskilled up to twenty-five, women fourteen to sixteen; and the families did not object to their women working here, as usually the father and brothers would be employed as well. The company provided houses in a village about two miles away and also gave the people free pasteurized milk.

All this he related with a just pride, but when we touched on more general matters his face grew long. Mérida was a wilderness of the soul, he said, there was no cultural or intellectual life whatever: only gossip. On finishing his day's work in the laboratory he went straight to his study and read alone for the rest of the evening. He lived in a small pretty house to the side of the factory, sharing it with seven or eight colleagues, all bachelors and mostly young: it was very agreeably furnished and even had a small well-stocked bar and a waiter, like a country club. Into this, as into a fortress, they all retreated in their leisure hours, isolating themselves from the heathen and making life as best they could. He spoke wistfully of Madrid, which he had been obliged to leave after the Civil War, and still more so of England, showing me photographs of London University groups, a wooden shield from an Oxford college and one from Cambridge, all happy trophies from a vanished past. He was a true Spanish intellectual with the fine ironic humour of that kind, the indecision, the yearning for "abroad," and the high ambitions for his own country which go together with a sense of their futility; and needless to say he told me that the Spaniard of today preferred football to bull-fighting, a statement not only untrue in itself but which places the man who makes it as surely as a derogatory remark about hunting does in England. His post in these remote pig-geries seemed hardly in keeping with his attainments.

He was good enough to arrange an appointment for me with the gentleman from Vigo, who held a position similar to his own in the local cork factory; and I was able to follow the long routine of cork-making from tree of the forest to champagne bottle. One whole department had to be given up to the labour of dyeing bright red the corks intended for Germany, a curious specification of which I inquired the reason.

"*Por capricho!*" my companion said wearily with a wave of his hand that classified the Germans for ever.

On the subject of Mérida he was still more eloquent than his colleague, having all the fire of youth behind him and further, as a standard of comparison, his birthplace, Vigo, beside which the glories of Madrid and England were evidently as nothing. It was terrible here, ghastly! Nothing of interest ever happened: the visit of the Lope de Vega Company the other week had been a red-letter day to be dreamed of for months before and afterwards. In the normal way the recreation

of the people was to come out of doors in the cool of the
evening, stare at each other, have a drink or two and talk about
pigs, football and their neighbours. And this for three hundred
and sixty-five days of the year! It was well enough for the
local inhabitants, Extremadura being noted for its brutish igno-
rance and similarity to Portugal, but he and his wife (from
Vigo) were used to something *mas elevado.*

Vigo, ah Vigo! There was a city. There were splendid
buildings and fine streets, an instructed society and a cultivated
life. And the whole land of Galicia was lovely, cool and green,
for it was always raining there, just as in Ireland. Think of it!
he cried in his anguish: rain every day! I asked if he had
ever been to Ireland and he replied that he had not, but he
knew he should feel at home in the country, what with the
rain and all being Celts together. As I had never yet been to
Vigo or Galicia, the wonderful absurdity of his remarks was
lost on me at the time: in the days to come I was to savour it
greatly. I left the passionate boy on the factory steps, glowering
at the yellow sun-baked plains of Extremadura, haunted perhaps
by a vision of eternal mist and rain: he had kindly given me a
bag of corks in various sizes to take away, but as there were no
bottles to go with them the gift was nugatory.

My visit here had been made first thing after breakfast,
which meant at about half past ten, and by now the sun was
climbing up with its usual wicked *brio.* All that remained on
the program this morning was to have my hair washed and
to change some money at the bank, but it seemed a great
way beyond my powers. The sweat was coursing down my
frame in tiny rivers and falling in drops on the ground; and
once when a little beggar boy confidently laid his hand on
my arm I was ready to scream at the heat of his touch. It
looked as if my two intellectual friends had been a little severe
with the people of Mérida. Living in this inferno, how were
they to be blamed if their thoughts were not always fixed on

philosophy and *belles lettres?* After only forty-eight hours of it I had become a mindless, palpitating mass. With awe I remembered the despatches written by Wellesley from this hellish region in the August of 1809: among all his complaints of the shilly-shallying of the Spanish Government, the broken promises of the Spanish staff, the fleetness, in the wrong direction, of the Spanish soldier and the non-delivery of food and provender for man and beast, the weather was not so much as mentioned. Indeed, his favourite threat was to march the army off at speed to Portugal: a man of iron if ever there was one.

Puling specimen of the same heroic race, I now tottered into what appeared to be a café, in the principal street; and here the natives of Mérida were to show that whatever they lacked it was not sweetness of manners. The orange juice I ordered was very promptly and courteously brought, and to my surprise cost only half the usual amount: equally surprising was that many of the tables were taken up by unescorted women, a thing I had never seen in a Spanish café before. It was only as I was going out that I learned from notices at the entrance that it was not a café at all, but a private club. No one had stared or passed remarks or resented the stranger's presence in any way; and it may be doubted if the experience of a foreigner who sat down in an English club—say, the Athenaeum—and ordered a drink would have been as comfortable.

Changing money in Mérida was not the simple affair that it might have been supposed. The external grandeur of Spanish banks is in great contrast to the shabbiness of our own, but there seems to be precious little money in them, or perhaps it is just that they hate to see it go. My cheques bore the name of an English bank known all over the world, but none the less were objects of the gravest suspicion here. They were examined, held up to the light and removed to the manager's office for comparison with a list of respectable banks. In time the clerk would come back and ruefully say that they could not be changed without a special authority from Madrid: no doubt the Bank was an illustrious one, but unknown to themselves: however, the Bank of Bilbao was only a few doors away. . . . Out with me, therefore, into the glaring sunshine once again. This pantomime was enacted in three or four establishments until at last, in the very Bank of Spain itself, I emotionally declared that I should have to spend the rest of my life in a debtor's jail; and at this Spanish humanity intervened and, having taken copious notes from my passport and informed themselves of my past, present, future and permanent addresses, they smilingly gave me the money, a matter of twenty pounds.

The amount of time the little businesses of every day take up in Spain is past believing. I was now to spend three hours or so at the hairdresser. This was not due to any incompetence, for hairdressers here are nearly all good and many a little rustic girl seems able to do as well as all but the best at home. The delay arose from their having fixed an appointment which bore no relation whatever to the time at which they proposed to make a start. Come at twelve! they had cried with enthusiasm: forgetting that at twelve all hands would be busied about the heads of five small girls, undergoing a permanent wave by a system long discarded elsewhere and who now sat in a ring looking like dispirited African warriors. And indeed there was a little sense of Africa in the whole place, with its weird utensils and the great basket in the middle of the floor that was piled with human hair, like the remains of some outrageous sacrifice. After an age or two the five little girls stood up, sleek and crinkly as newborn lambs, and I made a determined rush for the only washbasin. But at that moment a pretty young woman entered the room, blushing and smirking. She had no appointment, she explained, but was to be married at twelve o'clock on the following day and this, as was felt

109

by all but me, entitled her to precedence. She was at once and lovingly enthroned, object of the keenest sympathy and interest of every soul in the place, and so conscious of herself and her imminent translation as to feel every odd glance that fell on her like a blow; and as soon as all particulars of the groom, ceremony, banquet and honeymoon had been prized from her, a general discussion of the married state from a feminine point of view took place.

I lunched, therefore, at half past four with an excellent appetite. To sit under the dryer had been most refreshing, as even when turned up to the highest degree it was a great deal cooler than the air outside. But after the meal as I looked from my bedroom window on to the dead square below, the men asleep in the shade of the trees, the panting, exhausted animals, an awful foreboding arose. How much longer could it be borne? Surely I was mad to have come? I thought bitterly of Madame D'Aulnoy, that enterprising armchair traveller of the seventeenth century, whose brilliant volume of *Travels into Spain* was crowned by all critics of discernment, including Taine and Sainte-Beuve; and who had had the sense to compose it without ever setting foot in the country. The fake was not discovered for two hundred years: surely a sign of hope for us all? But it was too late, I should have laid the plans before: now there was nothing for it but to try and sleep until darkness came and for a few hours at least life would be more or less tolerable.

12

PERVERSELY, the coach for Trujillo left at six in the afternoon
instead of the cool of the morning as usual; and we were no
sooner fairly under way than violent, tearing pains in my stomach announced that it had put up with as much of my nonsense
as it expected to.

The road led once more through the splendid rolling plains
of this region, now no longer tawny or yellow but ashen, as
if the sun had bleached the last drops of colour away; and
here too were the curious jagged mountains that so abruptly
leaped up against the horizon. Everywhere the people were
busy about the harvest, the banks of grain undulating for mile
after mile like dunes of pale sand, and the fine gold dust
from the chaff drifting about in the air and making everyone
sneeze. Sometimes the grain was trodden out by horses only
and sometimes a man was drawn along after them on a kind
of sleigh; and I never saw a tractor at this or any time.

About halfway between Mérida and Trujillo is a tiny village
called Miajadas, where Christ might have stopped, even as he
stopped at Eboli. Even in Spain it would be hard to find
more terrible, dull, hopeless poverty. Ragged women sat at
the doors of their hovels watching their dirty children listlessly
at play in the road, while the men had collected in the two
or three sordid bars, with the rickety worm-eaten tables and

111

grimy bead curtains across the entrance, near the bus stop. Wherever you looked were broken windows, cracked peeling façades and pits in the road: here and there an attenuated fowl scratched wildly in the crumbling soil and found nothing. Yet the old men and women, with suffering deeply etched in their faces, came to smile at the travellers and wave them on their journey.

After Miajadas the coach mercifully regained the smoothly surfaced high road to Madrid. Now it passed through mighty prairies and olive groves in which horses, mules and herds of cattle roamed at will. No fence of any kind was there to hinder them crossing the road when they felt disposed, a circumstance that motorists had to take into account. As the sun went down we reached the Sierra de Montanchez and began steadily climbing, at which the engine of the bus protested a great deal: and now for about twenty minutes to the left side of the way was a most magnificent panorama of those flowing rippling corn-steppes that mingled in the fading light with the sky, until one could hardly tell which was which. Droves of the famous black pigs wandered over the face of them, grunting and rooting. At last on a hill directly ahead stood Trujillo, the church at the peak of it.

On arriving at the Fonda Pizarro I was too ill to do anything but go straight to bed, in the usual tiny oven, which here had the particular disadvantage of being right beside the clock-tower of a church; and the clock itself had the further particularity of striking every hour twice over, in a tremendously emphatic boom that called to mind a certain species of bore. What with this, the commotion the storks made with their wings the whole night through, a noise oddly like the flapping of wet sails, and the subversive activities of my stomach, I never closed an eye.

Of all the kind women I met in Spain, and these were many, the old white-haired *padrona* of the Pizarro was the kindest. In the morning I asked her to give me the name of a doctor and with many exclamations of pity she ran to the telephone to make an appointment, and even told one of the maids to bring me to it; being like most Spaniards unshakably convinced that no foreigner has any mind at all. The doctor's house was barely two hundred yards away, but the distance seemed much more, as the little maid was continually meeting with other little maids about their morning errands, when of course she had to stop and kiss, explain the purpose of our outing and disclose the awful details of my condition, while I leaned against the wall and shivered and sweated. In a place of this size they had probably all met each other just twenty minutes before, but it was an agreeable custom.

The doctor had his apartment in one of the larger, older houses of the town, a pleasant, high-roomed one with good pictures and a great many books. His wife nipped in to the waiting-room as I sat there, to examine me with that insatiable Spanish curiosity in personal affairs that somehow never offends. She was most friendly and polite, and did her best to look unconcerned when I confessed that I was travelling alone. Repeatedly she told me I ought to have come in April when Trujillo was fine and cool and there were beautiful *fiestas:* she plainly considered, as I did, my trip to be madness. Presently her husband opened his door and called, and having secured the greater part of my life's story she retired in satisfaction. The doctor was a charmer as well, despite the two-day beard on his chin, and his breath, which suggested that he lived mainly on cloves of raw garlic. It did not take him long to make the diagnosis: it was *nada:* all the matter was that I had been drinking the waters of the various towns I stayed in, a highly dangerous thing to do. Except, of course, in Trujillo, he added at once: the water of Trujillo could be drunk by man, woman and child with entire confidence: but in every other place one should keep to the bottled Solares. With that he wrote out a number of prescriptions, and charged me fifty pesetas: it was nothing at all and the medicines he ordered proved to be quite delicious. It is a curious thing that Spaniards, who will stoically endure all manner of painful things for which we should require an anaesthetic, seem to be rather babyish about their medicines and to want them all flavoured with chocolate or orange.

Meanwhile the good *padrona* of her own free will had moved my things into the largest and coolest room she had; and seating herself beside me as I lay on the bed she begged for a full report of the visit. She said that all the doctors in Trujillo were unusually clever, but the one she had recommended was the cleverest of the lot. Then she left the room, to return directly with a dish of little cakes which, she said, could not possibly do any harm as they were fresh baked and "*muy rico*." They tasted predominantly of olive oil, and she sat there smiling firmly until the last crumb was eaten.

In a short time I was well enough to be looking about me again. The little ancient city, thought to have been founded by Julius Caesar, had an immense, haggard, decayed charm. The *plaza* was dominated by a huge bronze statue, turned by weather and time to a lovely green, of the great Francisco Pizarro, the "fierce, false, cruel" conquistador of Peru: clad in armour and mounted on horseback he looks arrogantly down at the place of his birth and probably sees little of change in it. He was born in 1480 as the son of a local swineherd and is said to have been suckled by a local sow; but there are so many legends about the conquistadores, and they bear such a pronounced family likeness, that it would be rash to depend on this. Green trees line the little *plaza* and there is a round pool of green water in the middle of it, on the stone banks of which the boys and girls collect at evening and chatter blithely away until far into the night. To one side are the biggest and most frequented cafés, the hub of Trujillo's social life, and on the other side is the market, with repulsive oddments of fly-blown meat laid out on slabs, piles of cucumber and marrow and strings of garlic, and a crockery store, where breakfast cup, holy image and chamber-pot all jostle each other companionably on the one shelf.

An unusual feature of the city is the number of fine buildings that once were the residences of the wealthy and powerful; for in comparison with other countries Spain is poor in domestic architecture. The men who came back from Peru fat with the spoils of conquest housed themselves in a manner befitting their achievement. Today they are shells, melancholy reminders of vanished greatness: some are empty, others inhabited by folk of lesser degree: one *palacio* with a particularly splendid doorway which bore the notice "This building is the property of Their Excellencies the Lord Dukes of San Carlos" now had as its tenant the clerk to the Town Council. And all give the sense of utter decrepitude, as if one were only to watch long enough and one would see the crumbling stones gently fall from them one by one.

From the ramparts of the *castillo* that crowns the hill there is an immense view of the tableland immediately round the city and the dark Sierras behind that: a landscape grim and bare, identical with that which met the eyes of Pizarro and his friends four and a half centuries ago. For nothing appears to have been added since that time: all is emptiness and silence. An old lady came out and offered to show me the Patron of Trujillo, La Virgen de la Victoria, who had once appeared on the very spot. She began to describe the apparition, but she had not a tooth in her head and I soon lost the thread of the narrative. Both Virgin and Child wore crowns of gold set with diamonds that were top-heavy and tilted awkwardly over their eyes: these had been given them only two years ago, the old lady told me. "*Una padrona muy mona,*" she said, gazing at the doll with a fond pride: the expression *mona* (monkey) being used, by some quirk of the Spanish fancy, to indicate particular beauty. Every night the patron is floodlit and may be seen from the *pueblo* beneath glowing in a pool of light, a modern touch to which the people refer with great satisfaction. Her little chapel had been completely restored and was wonderfully kept, and there was apparatus for floodlighting all round the old castle, with a row of businesslike switches along one of the walls. Besides the old lady there was only one ancient custodian in a spotless white uniform whose duties appeared to consist of rising and bowing as one arrived and again as one left.

Near by is the Church of Santa Maria, surrounded by other ancient edifices with the coats of arms and fragmentary stone carvings that make the façades of Trujillo so charming. It was shut, and the place had the aloof, uninterested air of one that has served its turn. In a quiet corner of the holy precincts two little boys were squatting, their trousers down, while a third wearing a battered tophat several times too large for him danced and sang to keep them entertained. Everywhere the storks were perched: they seem to spend the whole summer balancing peg-legged on towers and looking stupid, apart from making little practice flights to keep fit for the day when they should wing off to Africa and perch and look stupid there. I looked about for signs of life. A few yards away was a hovel with a tiny garden shaded from the sun by an overhanging vine, on which were fat bunches of grapes on the turn from green to gold; and from the interior came the blithe music of women's voices all speaking at once and accompanied now and again by the bass grunt of a pig, like a cello among the flutes. In answer to my knock the women all came pouring out and one of them at once darted away, screaming that she would fetch El Viejo.

A group of infernal children now collected about me, shrieking for money. I gave a peseta to the biggest and told him to buy sweets for them all; but he welshed at once, fleet as a greyhound, while the others howled recriminations after him and further claims against myself. El Viejo hobbled up with the enormous keys of the church in his hand and followed by the woman, who led along an aged crone soliciting alms. These were given, but the sight of the money roused the children to frenzy, and El Viejo and I had to cut and run for the church door, which he hurriedly and with trembling fingers unlocked while I beat the marauders off: then, breathless, we pushed inside and barred ourselves against them, they pounding on the door and bawling threats and obscenities as it might have been the *jacquerie*.

Substantial repairs and restorations—at the expense, El Viejo said with glee, of the Government in Madrid—were in progress, although the workmen were nowhere to be seen. We had to pick our way over piles of wood and stone, under ladders and through ghostly dust-covers that fell about us like collapsing tents. For a church in so diminished and exhausted a community it had its full share of beautiful things, above all a magnificent *retablo* by Gallegos of scenes from the life of Our Lady, splendid with blue and gold, and in a side chapel two lovely paintings of Morales. But apart from these everything spoke rather of earthly glory and earthly dominion: it was a temple of Spanish might rather than a house of God, and thus a fit object for the benevolence of Madrid. The arms of the great local families looked arrogantly down from the walls, their tombs were scattered on the floor: Vargas, Torres, Pizarro, Calderón, Altamira, name after resounding name. In one chapel that seemed entirely given up to the memory of the Conquistador there was an amazingly hideous wreath of artificial flowers and leaves with a sash in the Peruvian colours and the dedication—

El Peru
a Don Francisco Pizarro
1541–1941

1541 being the year of his death by the hand of the treacherous Herrada. We stood, El Viejo and I, contemplating for a while the Spain that had been before slowly returning to the one that was, the filthy, screaming children and the stinking streets, the languor, the hopelessness, the deprivation.

It would have been pleasant to take another turn about the castle wall, but the children made it impossible. I think I never saw a meaner bunch of brats. The instant El Viejo opened the door of the church they fell on me, screaming and trying to pull my bag away; and when at last the idea sank into their brains that there was to be no more money they baited me as if I had been an animal. A stone would catch me in the small of my back and as I whirled about to discover the culprit, another small fiend would creep up and jab me viciously with a pointed stick, while the rest kicked my shins with a will: it is amazing how much a horny little toe can hurt. There were only eight or nine of them, tiny, stunted, ragged creatures under the rule of a *cacique* who appeared to be not more than six or seven years old; but I was soon in headlong flight down the stone steps of the Way of the Cross that led to Trujillo, and did not mind who knew it. About halfway down the blessings came to a halt, as if before some invisible line that bounded their territory, and slowly withdrew to their lairs, bawling insults over their shoulders. It was now the turn of the *jeunesse dorée*, for as I limped into the *plaza* a phalanx of little girls in white silk dresses and with white satin bows in their hair raised a howl of *"Fea! Fea! Fea! Fea!"* which they continued chanting in huge enjoyment until a lady passing on her way to church bade them hold their peace. To be ugly, she told them, surveying me compassionately, was a misfortune, but not a sin: and it was rudeness to mention it.

I went across to one of the cafés and asked for a glass of *horchata*. This is a drink made from almonds, of a sweetish and insipid flavour, but enormously refreshing and a capital thing for a roasting day; but the waiter gravely shook his head.

"You don't want that," he informed me.

"Is there no *horchata* here?"

"Of course," he said impatiently. "We have it. But you don't want it. You wouldn't *like* it. Now then. How about a lemonade? Or some coffee?"

"As it seems best to you." He turned it over in his mind, and fetched a glass of lemonade.

It was eight o'clock of the afternoon and by no means time for Trujillo to start drinking. The only people in the cafés were the half-dozen old men who remained there all day long. Nor did the *plaza* itself offer a great deal in the way of diversion. Men occasionally strolled across the square, furiously scratching the fork of their trousers, one of the most characteristic of Spanish sights. Now and again a creaking cart would lumber across it, drawn by resigned black cows with a triple row of bells under their chins like a dowager's pendant: or one of the large wagons peculiar to the region, with a wide curved hood and four horses, that made one think of a Western film. Over the way outside the market a man was overcome, by the heat, or by emotion, or because he had been done down in a negotiation, and the white-coated Guardia Civil patted him kindly on the back and a servant-girl ran out of a house to him with a jug of water in her hand. One of the mules kicked another and was banged on the bottom for it by his owner. Suddenly, like visitors from another planet, a big French motor car sailed into the square and three excessively elegant ladies got out and came to the café. That rigid disciplinarian, the waiter, moved slowly across to find out what their intentions were and an argument followed.

"You wouldn't like it," I could hear him repeating.

The French ladies got huffily back into their motor and drove away. After that there was a pause in the flow of incident. Staring vaguely about me, I saw an announcement that *Mrs. Miniver* was to be shown in the cinema tonight, and that she was *tolerada*. So the Spaniards were a tolerant people after all.

Was it my duty to attend the performance and note the audience's attitude to that most singular creation? If it were, I should leave it undone. For a while I meditated on the fine distinction between *tolerado* and *autorizado* and amused myself by trying to picture the immensely confident people who were able to make it. Presently we had what was quite a windfall: two very distinguished gentlemen, one with a white spade beard and both with rosettes in their buttonholes, entered and sat in profound silence beside an old countryman wearing a stiff-brimmed hat and the stubble of several days. They were good for twenty minutes' speculation at least. And then there was a further stroke of luck, for the waiter came up and fell into conversation. Having fairly tamed me, he could afford to be handsome, and he unbent still more when he learned that I was not French. He did not in the least care for French people and did not mind if he never saw any. There were no historical or political grounds for it, it was merely his *sentimiento;* but England was another case entirely, and he inquired after Mr. Churchill. All these little things added up to make one's Trujillo evening; and if one lived here they presumably made one's life. By their pleasant means the time slipped gently away until darkness fell, the square came alive and far above the *pueblo* the "monkey" little Patron could be seen glowing on her altar.

Alas! I was to have an opportunity of savouring the minutiae of Spanish provincial life more intensely yet. The next stage on the route was to Plasencia and I had too readily assumed that a bus would be going in that direction every day. It went only twice a week and now it appeared I had just missed one; and for three grilling days I alternated between my bedroom, studying maps and reading Spanish novels, and one or the other of the cafés, hoping for some sensational occurrence, such as a dog-fight. In a society less rigid one might have been able to make the acquaintance of a few of the inhabitants, but the Spaniard clings to formal introductions and due observances and, above all, prefers ample warning beforehand in which to prepare his mind for the approach of anything strange. The only company to be had was that available in the *fonda* itself, and this was limited more or less to men concerned in the pig trade who came and went. But there was one old priest, a schoolteacher, living there all the year round and he, with his long, brown, Castilian face and white hair and his sweet manner, was a delightful person. We came to know each other fairly well because the meals were never ready for three quarters of an hour at least after the official time, and we used to talk to each other while we waited. His favourite theme at present was the performance of *Julius Caesar* at Mérida, to which he would ever and again revert, quite carried away and reliving it in his imagination. *Estupendo! Maravilloso!* And his eyes would glow and his hair stood on end. But the instant the waitress bustled in with the meal, with the owner beaming anxiously from the doorway as if to say, "There you are! Only a minute or two behind!" he would break off at once, often in the middle of a sentence; then he would cross himself devoutly, say his grace, tuck his napkin in behind the second button of his soutane and apply himself to his food in unbroken silence.

13

EVEN IN SPAIN you will hardly find country grander than that between Trujillo and Plasencia. The way ran across a range of mountains whose sides towered sheer above the road in vast, smooth faces of rock, grey with the blazes of yellow or orange lichen, or in strata like a pile of enormous blocks laid together on their sides: and over little mountain bridges with the River Tagus purling and foaming over its rocky bed far below. Now and again at a turn of the road the great toothed ridge of the Sierra would suddenly offer itself head on, shimmering silvery in the morning sun. The sense of wildness and desolation was overpowering, and there was nowhere a touch of softness or grace to be seen.

The bus was a comic turn, even for the Spanish countryside. The plaintive whine of the engine as the driver put it to still another appalling gradient was most affecting: indeed, after each lengthy halt on the road there was always a doubt as to whether it would start again and invariably the conductor had to go to the rescue with the crank. Likewise at every pause, or even stopping for the purpose at lonely mountain cottages, he begged a bowl of water to put fresh heart into the fuming radiator. The doors on each side flew incontinently open one after the other, with danger of losing the passengers crammed against them; and as usual the upper and lower parts of the vehicle strained and swayed in different directions, as if unconnected.

Many days had been lost in Trujillo and it was now the 7th of July; and as I had to be in Santiago de Compostela for the Feast of St. James on the 25th, I had regretfully decided to leave Plasencia out and press immediately on to Salamanca. There was time only for breakfast and the briefest look at the Cathedral. In it, no doubt to cheer and encourage the heavy-laden, was a captivating broadsheet by the Capuchin Fray José Diego of Cadiz, called "La Reloj de la Muerte": a death's head grinned out of the face of a clock in the most comfortable way and edifying verses were wreathed around it. In Spain one is never allowed to forget death for more than five minutes. But then the sacristan came hobbling up and crossly told me to cover my head. As I had nothing better, he insisted I hold my notebook on it and in this ludicrous fashion we toured the holy place together. He himself spat freely on the floor from time to time. The choir-stalls were particularly fine, and the carvings, by Rodriguez Aleman, enchanting, especially those under the canonical seats: there was a sly humour in the fox preaching to the fowls, and a masterly irrelevance in the woman washing her legs in a basin. A delicious book waits to be written on the naughty and unsuitable motifs tucked away in the shadowy corners of sacred buildings.

On the way to Salamanca, after the terrible scorching of Extremadura, it was agreeable to note the signs of a return to the north. The wheat here was not yet cut: poppies and cornflowers waved in the grass by the roadside, there were brambles in the hedge, orchards with tiny apples and pears hanging on the boughs, a lovely green blush on the earth; and, a magic sight, on the crests of the Sierra de Gredos three or four patches of snow. And in Salamanca itself, what happiness it was to get to the Hotel Monterrey and find a fierce gush of water in the taps! Entering a good hotel in Spain is a strange experience, as if one had left the country for a while. I filled the bath at once and lay in it for an hour, plunging and wallowing and grunting like a satisfied hippopotamus.

After so many rural rides it was exhilarating to be in a noble city again. Near the hotel was an excellent bookshop: I had almost forgotten such things existed, and in a kind of delirium bought three more novels, which I could not afford and for which there was no room in my luggage. There was also the latest number of *Insula*, the literary and philosophical review published in Madrid, which, as its somewhat provocative name suggests, is a little island of sophisticated intelligence in the contemporary Spanish desert. It was an article by Julian Marias dealing with aspects of Spanish bourgeois mentality, notably with that peculiar magnificent imperviousness which excited the wonder of less confident minds and offers, to the uncharitable, an alternative reason for the Spanish veneration of the Bull: "We know it all, what we don't know is bunk, we know (or pretend to know) just what we are and what we are about"; and for this Marias had coined the word *Solucionismo*, a definition of so wicked a beauty that never again would the frame of mind it describes have power to irritate.

While I was savouring it, the hotel page appeared with a letter on a salver: clearly the register was open to all for inspection. My Christian name leads many people on the Continent to suppose that I am titled, and the letter, inviting me to an exhibition of Spanish crafts and signed by "The Craftsmanship Managing Director for Salamanca," was properly deferential. A leaflet enclosed remarked: "The incomparable Spanish handicraft condenses in its works all the spirit of the race, the traditions of its history, the charm of its regions, the luminosity and the beauty of its flowers: a perfect spiritual sedative. Do not forget that any object may be termed wonderful if the matter of which it is formed has been transformed by the great sensibility of the

124

Spanish craftsman." And wonderful indeed the collection proved to be, on the gnome-and-toadstool level: vile fans, dreadful crucifixes, pottery with bunnies on it and fiddling musical boxes, all at extortionate prices. The star turn was a cognac bottle in gold and white china which burst into music when it was picked up: very likely the idea was to startle the customer into dropping it, when he could be charged. All was chi-chi and fuss, with nothing traditional, plain or beautiful anywhere, as if some of the informers and spies made redundant by the increasing stability of the régime had been directed into cultural activities.

There was to be never a dull moment in Salamanca. No sooner had I returned from this dismal expedition than the page appeared again with another envelope on his salver. Now the story ran as follows:

"In Salamanca presently there is something new which cannot be found in Tourist Guides, but can indeed be of interest to the Tourist: the work of 'Brick by Brick' which is being constructed with no other economic basis than the voluntary offerings of the people of Salamanca.

"This is, in effect, a large building of four sections to serve the social needs of the suburb of Prosperidad. This is one of the largest suburbs of Salamanca.

"If you wish to leave 'your brick' as a remembrance of your visit to Salamanca, you can put your offering in the box in the lobby of your hotel or deposit it at the place of construction: Reverendo Padre Basabe, Obra 'Ladrillo a Ladrillo,' Paseo de San Antonio.

Plain brick	*1 peseta*
Silver brick	*5,000 pesetas*
Gold brick	*25,000 "*
Diamond brick	*50,000 "*

Thank you."

125

The naïve effrontery of this gave me a good deal of pleasure. Further information was that the cornerstone had been laid on the Feast of St. Joseph, 1952, and that "bricks" had been freely offered every day since. For this reason it was called the Miracle of St. Joseph, and it seemed only unfortunate that St. Joseph could not have made a job of it and turned the plain bricks into diamond ones. The leaflet had pictures as well, to illustrate the steady march of Progress. "Where yesterday there was nothing . . ." was the caption to one, showing six or seven hideous new buildings. I went to see the Miracle, with its ugly new church, its canteen, its children's center, all the bleak outlines of Prosperidad. In front of it stood a bent old beggar whining mechanically to the passersby as he wrenched his shirt to one side to show the horrid stump of an arm.

Further efforts of the régime to prove itself worthy of the past were to be seen in the Gran Via, a thoroughfare in the process of construction, mercifully apart from the beauties of the town. The style generally adopted might be described as Fascist Box, of which the new Palacio de Justicia was a particularly grandiose example: the more hollow the proceedings, evidently, the more impressive the building. In the Ministry of Information, another large box, sat one of those sharp Spanish business ladies who appear to believe that rudeness is a mark of efficiency. I had to consult her about hiring a motor car for the following day, and also about various places I wished to visit. She gave me the address of a garage which proved not to exist, and declared that the Sanctuary of the Peña de Francia was closed to the public, which turned out to be wrong as well. This lady was in charge of Tourism. Guided, as one usually is in the end, by random citizens, I found a garage with cars for hire: and the owner promised to be with me the next day at the crack of dawn, which means in Salamanca about nine o'clock.

Punctually he appeared, a cheerful, vocal person of fifty or so with a good, satiric turn of mind and phrase, dressed in a white silk shirt and freshly creased trousers and obviously determined to enjoy the day as much as anyone. As we drove out of the city, which seemed as we left it behind to perch on its hill like a beautiful bird, he answered my questions with great candour. Life in Spain was growing a little easier in some ways: there was more liberty of thought and speech and assembly. But you couldn't eat liberty. Economic injustice was as great as ever, and the schemes of the Government merely intended to catch the eye. The peasants were the worst off of all: in the summer they worked seven days a week from sunrise to sunset and earned little enough; in the winter they were either stood off or put on short time, when they had to manage the best they could. But the great landed proprietors were more comfortably placed than ever. Alone in Europe the Spanish aristocracy had maintained and even strengthened their position, and that without always deserving to. Of the three great local families, two were Marqueses and one a Conde: we could see their land now on each side of the road, stretching away into the distance for mile upon mile. The Republicans ought to have won the war, and so they would have done with a few good generals. Some of them had made very bad mistakes, but these had been greatly exaggerated since. The victorious are always in the right, he observed gaily. His brother-in-law, who had six little children, had been taken out and shot long after the fighting was over, for nothing at all.

Now, perhaps, feeling that he had done his share, he began to press me for details of the various makes of English cars, their speeds, prices, performances and gas consumption, and seemed very much surprised that I knew nothing at all about the matter.

Having some little experience of Spanish tourist offices, I asked him to drive up to the Santuario de la Peña de Francia on the chance that we should be allowed in. It belongs to the Dominicans, who use it as a holiday place in the summer, coming up a few at a time from the parent house in Salamanca. In winter snow makes the mountain road impassable, and the winds and the frost are so bitter that, despite the great thickness of the walls, there has to be much repairing done every spring. It sits on a peak 1,725 meters high and the road that curls round the mountain up to it is eleven kilometers long, running first through woods of evergreen oak in which there are wild animals rarely found in Spain, wolves, foxes, wild boar and *"animales volatiles de distintas familias,"* my companion said, although he could not name the flying animals as we did not see any: then suddenly emerging from the green dusk it winds up a mountainside of boulders splashed with gay lichen and studded with thickets of golden broom, offering with every twist a new magnificent view of the surrounding peaks and plains. As we went climbing up our ears began to crackle and we felt the joyous lightheadedness that comes of mountain air. The driver burst into song and begged me, as we careered round hairpin bends with our wheels an inch from the side, to have no fear as he had never gone over yet.

When we reached the top, a young Dominican Father hastened out of the monastery to greet us. He led the way to the pilgrims' *hosteria*, where they served a breakfast of coffee, bread and butter and cherries. "Eat," said the driver in a guarded undertone. "Who knows what their lunch may be like?" The Father said that not only were visitors welcome, but we could have hardly chosen a better time to come, for on the following day the monastery was to be inaugurated with the final enthroning of the Virgin in her place of honour. Workmen were busy installing a radio, so that the High Mass the Bishop of Salamanca was going to sing could be heard all over the city; and the Minister of Justice and his wife had promised to come as *padrinos* of the ceremony. Pilgrims would come from far and wide, many of them starting late this evening and walking up the miles of flinty road barefoot in the darkness and bringing votive offerings in gratitude for cures or other favours:

mothers would carry their babies up to offer them to the Virgin. And in return for their devotion and support the Fathers had gone to some trouble to arrange a little treat for them. In the evening there was to be a bull-fight, a *pequeña novillada,* with one small bull, doubtless rather puzzled and cross, brought up the whole length of the road by truck, to be fought in a ring the size of a handkerchief by Jumillano. Who, I asked, was Jumillano? And the Father's grave brown eyes kindled. The great *novillero,* the famous boy, the rising star of the ring: as Manolete was in his early days, so was Jumillano now. He came, the Father added, from Salamanca. In reply to a further question he told us, with a gentle sigh, that of course the monks would not attend the spectacle.

While we ate our breakfast he described to us with a charming simplicity the miraculous origins of the monastery, which were unusually involved. For once no local shepherd or goatherd had had a finger in them. The Virgin had appeared far away in France to a man called Simon and told him that somewhere in an unspecified mountain was buried a statue of herself. For seven years he searched in all the countries of Europe and at last in 1434 he came to this place. As he was trying to get to sleep one night through the din made by some arguing woodcutters, the Virgin appeared again and said: "Simon, watch and do not sleep." He jumped up at once and called the woodcutters to him, who agreed that clearly he had come to the end of his road. They and the people of the locality all helped him dig until at last they found the statue in a cave: it was black, very ancient and Roman in style, and had been buried by Christians during the Moorish invasion. Simon at once set to work to build a chapel on the spot, and the Dominicans, as the largest community in Salamanca, took charge of it. In the reign of Philip II possession was granted to them by royal decree and a stone with the kingly and Dominican *escudos* was set up in the courtyard. The little gothic church had been built in 1589, together with the *hosteria* for pilgrims, now reconstructed. Down the centuries and through all the many vicissitudes of the community in periods of anticlericalism the statue had undergone many adventures, but had always been faithfully cared for by the people of the district and returned to its place as soon as might be: until in 1952 it was canonically crowned in Salamanca by the Papal Nuncio to the Eucharist Congress of Barcelona, Cardinal Tedeschini, in the presence of fifteen bishops and three Ministers.

I have ventured to cream the Father's story of its principal features, since the whole thing took an hour and ten minutes in the telling. When he had finished it he took us to see the statue in the sacristy, which was being dressed by nuns in frilly white petticoats encrusted with gold. More nuns were busy polishing up its crown, which was of real gold set with pearls and diamonds, the gift of the faithful. It had been almost entirely reconstructed by a Spanish sculptor and now had the face of a woman of the district, although black; but a little of the original wood remained in the body and the nuns pulled the petticoats aside to show an inch or two of splintery, decayed surface. On the wall near by hung a splendid matador's cloak of pale blue velvet decorated with gold embroideries, spangles and jewels, offered to the Virgin by the fighter Jumillano. From time to time into this devout atmosphere there floated down scraps of jazz or the notes of a soprano as the workmen tested their radio in the tower above.

The good young Father showed us everything: the church with mosaics behind the empty pedestal waiting to receive the Virgin, the cave where Simon the Frenchman found the statue, the underground chapel built there, very simple and bare with a good stone carving on the altar, the minor chapels of Santiago, San Andrés and El Christo, of whom statues had also appeared at one time or another although when it comes to appearing none, not Our Lord himself, can hope to compete with the Virgin in Spain; and the three great wells full of water collected from the snows of winter. And he proudly displayed as well the tiny, improvised bull-ring, in which it hardly seemed the bull would have room to charge or the matador to get out of his way, with the frailest of barriers round it and the whole perched on the very edge of a ravine.

For some reason, I thought of a peasant I once met who had described how just such a mountain retreat as this had been carried away by witches in the time of his grandfather; and I told the story to the Father, who shook his head with a smile.

"Ay! There is a lot of superstition among our people," he said indulgently.

"Now here," he remarked, leading us to another steep cliff on the other side, "is El Niño: so called because a child playing on it fell over the side and, as you can see, there is a drop of three hundred feet: but by the miraculous intervention of the Virgin, he was unhurt."

There was no need to wonder, as with churchmen I have sometimes wondered, if he believed in this himself; for in his anxiety to point out this or that beauty spot he was capering excitedly about on the very edge, clearly assured that if necessary the Virgin would extend the same facilities to him.

Presently he was called inside and we sat down on the crags to rest. To one side stretched away the huge, sunny plains of Castile, to the other the countless blue peaks of the Sierra, whose range links up with others in an almost unbroken chain from the boundary of Portugal across Madrid to the Pyrenees. There were wonderful butterflies here, huge velvety creatures of black and white or orange and golden brown. The air was so quiet and still that the wings of swallows made a flailing noise as they circled and circled the peak. Another young Father, with the curious addition to his monk's habit of a peaked huntsman's cap, was dashing about the rocks like a mountain goat and pointing a gun at them, with shouts of "Boom! Boom!"

"What's the good of it? Why don't you put some shot into that gun?" asked a superior little boy who was accompanying him.

"Because I don't want to kill anything," the Father replied. "Boom! Boom! Boom!" he roared, levelling the gun again.

At noon there was a terrible burst of bell-ringing and rocket-firing, a foretaste of the splendid row that could be expected tomorrow. We dawdled on the rocks, too content to speak, until a nun came to bring us into the *hosteria* for lunch. The workmen were already hard at work on their meal and, as we sat down, they shouted some kindly, fraternal warnings about the wine. When we had eaten we reluctantly made our farewells: I asked for the young Father who had given so generously of his time and information, and offered him a *limosna*.

"No, no, no!" he exclaimed in horror, shutting his eyes and putting his hands behind him.

Please.

"No! Never!"

These simple ejaculations were repeated a dozen times before he relented. "Well, then . . . is it for the Virgin?" he at last inquired, cautiously opening his eyes.

For whom else?

The driver, by now in full party vein and deeply appreciative of the audience, reversed the motor with spirit on the verge of the steepest drop of all and, applauded by monks, nuns and workmen, drove down the terrifying road like a lunatic.

We now went on to La Alberca. The curious thing about this place was the architecture: the houses are entirely northern and gothic in appearance, with the first floor, much timbered, jutting out over the one below and rising to a gabled point. It is as if some crazy little village from Hans Andersen had been plumped down in the heart of Spain. The Government has declared it a national monument in its entirety, and so none may build or pull down or, seemingly, repair. Everything was down-at-heel and lean-to, and there was a dreary atmosphere of bore-dom, poverty and "reservation" life. The main square, with filthy water running between its broken paving-stones, had one fly-infested café called the Bar Moderno and a tumbledown shack of a cinema (San José) and had been duly rechristened Plaza Generalisimo Franco.

It was a relief to get away from it and continue our way to the Batuecas. This was an ancient convent nestling in a valley as hot as a greenhouse, surrounded by trees and with a stream forking round two sides of its walls. I had been told that it was occupied by an Order of cloistered nuns and much hoped to be allowed to see it; but as the motor car drew up a curly-haired young peasant sprang up and barred our way with a crook, like an angel defending the gates of Heaven. The nuns had gone, he said, and in their place were hermit *frailes:* I could not pos-sibly enter; the Pope himself was powerless to authorize it. But, he went on, with a delightfully wicked look on his face, there was a way round to the back from which I could see over the wall, and one of the little boys standing round should show it to me. The last thing I wanted was to play Peeping Tom on friars engaged in holy meditation; but the young peasant was as determined that I should go in by the back as that I should not do so by the front. The little boy was pressed into serv-ice, which he undertook with great reluctance, dolefully repeat-ing over and over again that the Fathers were not to hear of it. I was led to the fork of the stream and forced to make my way down it, leaping from boulder to boulder, skirting the trees on the bank with danger and difficulty, squeezing through a hole in a barbed-wire barricade in a manner unsuited to my age and weight and finally scaling the wall, which crumbled as I took hold of it: to be rewarded by a glimpse of a garden much overgrown with trees and shrubs and nothing else whatever. The peasant and the driver watched meanwhile from their safe positions with the gleeful terror of naughty children watching another accomplishing a "dare." When at last I scrambled back, the little boy lost some of his dreadful anxiety, and at the sight of a peseta even began to whistle.

From here we went on to the country of the Hurdes. A little way down the road two peasants signalled us to give them a lift. One should never expect to have a taxi to oneself for long in the Spanish countryside, for the peasants find the chance too good to miss. One of the men was old and wizened, with very bright eyes and a pretty gift of conversation: the other was young, with the face of a saint in an El Greco, with blue, child-like eyes and a very simple artless manner. As the car moved on, the old man remarked easily that he was a little tired, having walked eighty kilometres. There was no work in his own village, which was one of the poorest in Spain, but he had found a job scything crops in a distant place and now was returning home. He described his life with great simplicity, just as he accepted the lift, and commented on the Citroen as if he were in the habit of riding in one every day. I gave them cigarettes and offered the boy my box of matches, but as he put out his hand to take it the old man sharply rebuked him and told him not to waste my money. At this he drew out an immensely long, fat coil of orange-coloured wick with a mediaeval sort of flint at the end and coaxed from it a tongue of flame.

The village he lived in was a terribly poor one, in the very center of the Hurdes country. As we stopped so that the men could get out, a crowd immediately collected round the car. Some of them were of normal size and some were dwarfs: all in a curious way suggested deformity, and many were suffering from goiter. They stood there throwing oblique glances in our direction and smiling the withdrawn, sly smile of the half-witted. These were the Hurdes, the most debased and unhappy people in the whole of Spain.

The driver now suggested it was time to think of returning home and proposed an alternative route which would be more interesting for me, besides adding twenty-five shillings to the bill and enabling him to visit a friend of his. The friend was doctor to the Hurdes, and he lived in a compound with his wife, two *practicantes* and the local Guardia Civil. He was a gay, ebullient man of about thirty-five with a sweet, tranquil wife, whom he constantly sent here and there to fetch him handkerchiefs or other small articles of which, when she brought them, he made no use whatever, the whole caper being merely to impress us with his marital authority. The surgery and consulting-room he showed us made him feel ashamed, as the equipment had not been renewed since the post had been established in the reign of Alphonso XIII. Not one of his patients could afford to pay: there were ten thousand of the Hurdes and his practice was twenty kilometers across every way, some of it very rough country which he covered on horseback. Their compound was in a clearing in a pine wood and they walked us up to the point from which their best view was to be seen and then to the river where they bathed, this being one of their few diversions. They had no light and no running water: every drop they used had to be dragged up the hill from the river. It was a hard life, but he and his colleagues appeared gay and contented and entirely devoted to the poor creatures they were trying to help.

The driver seemed much disposed to settle down for the evening, but at last I was able to drag him away and persuade him to take me back to Salamanca. The return journey was made in absolute silence, as he had talked himself dry.

14

EVERY ONE of the persons to whom I had brought an introduction in Salamanca proved to be on his vacation. It was to be expected at this time of year that some of them would be, but it was a grievous blow to find no one at all. Nor was there much point in waiting about for them, as I was informed in every case that they would not return before the end of September. Holiday-making in Spain would appear to be arranged on the same principle as eating: it is done on the grand scale or not at all.

Architecture is a poor substitute for company. Yet there were many enjoyable hours to be spent wandering about this most beautiful city, where each building seems handsomer than the last and nearly all are built of the same apricot-coloured stone which glows in a wonderful way as if it drank in the sun and poured it out again. After the ardours of Extremadura the air struck deliciously cool, although the inhabitants were all groaning and exclaiming at the heat in the normal manner.

I inquired first for the Irish College, in order to settle a point that had arisen with a friend in the south. He had asserted that it was not Irish at all, but English: the Irish were at Valladolid; and with the fertile imagination of the novelist he drew a word-picture of the English candidates to be found there, sleek, purring and sophisticated. Nor could he be shaken by the fact of its certainly being known as the Colegio des Irlandeses, merely detecting in this a stroke of particular subtlety. It turned out to be neither. A melancholy old woman with a sharp yellow face peering out of a bundle of black garments said it was now a School of Theological Studies for priests of the Pontificate. She allowed me to stand in the exquisite little patio and look at the carvings on the rosy walls, but clucked a warning as I made for the stairs which led to the gallery.

"The Fathers are all up there," she cried, as if they were roosting fowl. She next conducted me to the chapel where there was a lovely *retablo* and ceiling and a decorative balcony supported by black and gold legs of such delicacy that they might have been Japanese. To each of the limited treasures on view the melancholy woman allotted a space of time which she severely limited as well; and when she deemed it enough she marched to the door and stood contemplating the street in a way that was unmistakable.

The New Cathedral, begun in 1513 and finished a couple of centuries later, is an unusual one, for the building of it luckily used all the money available and there was none left to clutter up the interior with lavish adornments. And perhaps it is not too fanciful to see reflected in that interior the change of religious sentiment in Spain within the two hundred years. For the superb west door outside is carved in rich and elaborate groups all leading the eye up to the figure of Christ crucified, which, smaller than some of the figures below, yet marvelously dominates the whole and claims recognition as the very core and center of the Faith. The conception here is still the mediaeval and masculine. *Mais nous avons changé tout ça.* Inside, it is unmistakably the temple of the Virgin: on the High Altar she is receiving the crown of heaven, and the side chapels are mainly hers, named for Our Lady of the Pillar, of Lourdes, of Solitude. I saw only two Christs, one ignobly pushed to the side with

137

long, artificial hair hanging limply from its head, a scarred and bleeding body and three skulls thrown at the foot of the Cross: the other in the chapel of San Expedito, a curious, bony, mis-shapen little figure like a wood-carving of some African jungle god. There is no doubt that the Virgin becomes ever more ex-alted in this country, gradually ousting the Christ except as Baby: at last, one can only surmise, it surely will end in the rele-gation of the Trinity to a role like that of the archangels, if not in its entire suppression.

In spite of their lack of money the chapter had been able to rise to a magnificent *coro*, the Twelve Apostles at the far end being particularly fine; and a homely air was imparted to the whole by the spittoons placed at intervals between the Canoni-cal seats. Here again I was turned out in a hurry as the Canons were about to sing their Hours, which they did at top speed as if the devil were behind them, some making even better time than others.

In front of one of the chapels was a fat drum with a strainer fitted across the top and into this the people tipped offerings of oil, a novel form of alms which I had not seen before. Whether it was olive oil for frying the Canons' fish or paraffin for keep-ing the lamps alight, or perhaps a mixture of the two, I cannot say.

One of the finest things in Salamanca, or for that matter in Spain, is the Plaza Mayor, which has an air of the Piazza San Marco about it: the sense of strength with lightness, the feeling of space created by beautifully just proportion, the noble arches and delicate, decorative façades; and it further has a charm to itself in the exquisite colouring of the stone. And something is always happening here: all day long it is the liveliest spot in the town and at night, when the cafés fill, the lanterns hanging from the arches burn and the air is rent with the shrill whistles of the police, it becomes like a scene from some enormous play. The young man now being smothered with kisses by all the members of the family in turn, including the male, must, you think, be newly returned from a concentration camp in Siberia: in fact, he is a cousin whom they haven't seen for a day or two and who chanced to pass their table en route to his own. And there is a little girl in a pink frock serenely perched on the handlebars of her father's motor-bicycle as he threads a way at top speed through the pedestrians, while the whistles shriek at him like peacocks and no one seems to get hurt. Wide-awake babies consume, until far into the night, astonishing quantities of lemonade and ice cream. And everywhere are boys and girls, not in the grim segregation described by those writers who patiently reiterate the truths of twenty years ago rather than use their own two eyes, but merrily laughing and talking together.

A delightful characteristic of Spanish cities is the village atmosphere that clings about them: the life of field and stable seems never far away. Ten minutes' walk from the New Cathedral and across the Roman Bridge you appear to be in the heart of the country. This Sunday evening great flocks of herds and goats had assembled on the far bank, while the owners prepared to camp for the night in readiness for a market tomorrow. An old iron pot or so and a little sacking to sleep on appeared to be the extent of their equipment. And on the near bank were dozens of picnicking families, with here and there a stray sheep wandering about between them with a puzzled look on its woolly face. At one point a complete dinner table had been set up on trestles, round which some dozen middle-class people were eating a large hot meal and beside which three old serving-women crouched as they waited to carry everything home again. It was a beautiful scene, with the slim young poplar trees shivering above the shivering waters of the weir, the little islands of grass touching the river with green and the bright reflections of children's dresses in the water, while the fading light of the sun bathed everything, Cathedral, bridge, beasts and merry-makers, in a pure gold.

The hotel in which I was staying was the most expensive but one in the place: twice already it had inconvenienced me with its misinformation on matters that clearly were in its province to know, and it was now to surpass itself. At five thirty next morning the telephone rang and a voice said I should get up at once if I wanted to catch the six-thirty coach to Zamora; and not till I had dressed and packed and sleepily gone down to the hall did the owner of the voice bethink him that in fact the coach left at six thirty in the afternoon. There was not, there never is, a word of apology on these occasions: an expression of haughty indifference comes over the face, the lower lip is pushed forward and the statement is repeated, prefaced with a *"Parece que"*—it would appear that—as if fresh details of the matter had suddenly and unexpectedly come to light. After the usual vain exclamations of fury, I said that at least there would have to be breakfast.

"Breakfast!"

Yes, breakfast.

The wooden-defensive attitude slowly gave place to the justifiably-indignant. Not content with coming down at all hours, the man's face seemed to say, she now must clamour for breakfast at six o'clock. Foreigners.

"If you will take a seat in the dining-room, breakfast will be served very shortly."

I had sat there for the best part of an hour before I smoked his little ruse. He raised his head and smiled cruelly as I swept past him to the street. On the pavement outside stood a policeman lost in admiration of his clean white gloves, whom I asked to direct me to a workman's café: but he merely looked astonished, as if there were no such thing as a workman in Salamanca. I went off to explore, my stomach grumbling peevishly at every yard, and presently the Guardia tore after me to say he had heard of a dairy near the Cathedral where they sold hot milk in the early morning. Leaving his beat to shift for itself, as well he might, for there was not a soul abroad, he led the way commandingly through the narrow streets until we came to the establishment he had in mind, which proved to be a sweet-shop piled high with nougat, candied oranges, lemons, pears, and caramels abhorrent to see at any time of the day; and with a bar of sweet, gritty chocolate I had to be content.

On returning to the hotel I found the night porter wreathed in smiles. The fact that he would have died sooner than admit his mistake did not prevent him from feverishly trying to undo it the instant my back was turned; and he had now discovered, and offered with a magnificent air of having known what was best all along, an autocar leaving for Zamora at nine fifteen. We took leave of each other with many compliments and expressions of esteem and on my part apologies for a foolish irritability which could be put down to distress at having to leave Salamanca at all.

The autocar was like a small, uncomfortable country bus unaccountably fixed on railway lines. Beside me sat a priest of a somewhat jaundiced complexion, with an ample picnic basket on his knee from which he refreshed himself with beakers of red wine, bread and butter and apricot jam.

"I have to eat this in the morning," he explained, "for I am on a diet. There is something the matter with my inside."

He then examined me closely on my own affairs, and urged me on no account to leave Leon out of my itinerary. If Leon was not in the book, he should not read it. He himself was from Leon. On my observing that things seemed to have slightly improved in the country over the last years he said yes, he thought so and particularly in Leon. They had recently built a *plaza de toros* there, a clear sign of progress; and he was very glad of it, for to his way of thinking there could never be too many *plazas de toros*.

"How many fights have *you* seen altogether?" he shot at me then, with a certain truculence of manner. I thought perhaps thirty, and he received the information benignly. "Then you may write about it," he said. "After thirty fights you may decently say a little."

His mouth was wide open to receive another wedge of bread and apricot jam when a thought so arresting came to him that he postponed the operation.

"If anyone tells you fighting is dying out and football taking its place, you mustn't believe it," he cautioned. "Football is rather popular these days; it would take too long to explain why. It will pass. I don't care for it at all, especially rugger: it is so horribly rough."

In Zamora there was time only for luncheon and a brief visit to the Cathedral before going on to Sanabria, the last stop before the promised rains of Galicia; and I did not regret it, for the place had a look of dust and decay and there seemed to be even more than the usual amount of unhappy or crippled people. The constant tapping of the sticks of the blind was a reminder of it, as the tick of a clock reminds one of the passing of time. Outside the Cathedral with his back against the wall a beggar sat, exposing a terrible leg swollen to many times its size, smooth and dark purple like an enormous eggplant, and wearily turned his head from side to side as the people went by without so much as a glance. The indifference of Spaniards to the suffering of others, apparently so cruel, may be due to the sheer mass and weight of it in their country: anything they did or gave would only be a drop in the sea; and after a time one feels oneself growing calloused too by despair at it.

The Cathedral was a fine building with a splendid Byzantine cupola, known as the Pearl of the Twelfth Century; but unhappily the choir-stalls and side chapels were all bolted and barred, nor could the guardian be induced to come and open them, as, with a large part of the male population, he was enjoying the spectacle of a burst water-main in the square a little way off. The precious water was cascading away down a side street while children splashed and paddled in it with shrieks of delight and the men looked on with a mixture of amusement and dismay. Two props of the Municipality, booted and helmeted like comic firemen, appeared, and after discussion tapped the pipe severely with an axe; and this had the typically *contraproducente* effect of causing the jet to spring several feet higher in the air, so that it now looked like a Sunday fountain. At last the officials stalked away, shrugging and gesticulating, at which the torrent suddenly stopped of its own accord, as if weary of the joke; and the crowd slowly dispersed, smiling reminiscently as people smile when they leave the theatre.

I had been told on no account to miss Sanabria, said to be one of the most beautiful places in this part of Spain. A very smart new *coche de línea* brought us there in a matter of three hours, through country steadily growing more northern in appearance. The sheep and goats looked fatter and sleeker, and there were green grass and green trees, with fields of potato and carrot, and orchards; and, most remarkable of all, many children wore shoes. On arriving at La Puebla de Sanabria, however, I could discern none of the special beauties promised and on inquiring for them was told that they were fourteen kilometers away; and that there was neither bus nor train. Nor, they said, if I drove there by taxi should I find anywhere to sleep.

But I thought it was a very famous beauty spot?

Ah yes, indeed, they said: so it is.

As the night was coming on there was nothing for it but to drive out to the Albergue de Turismo, a little distance from the Puebla and apparently still in the process of building. The foyer was wonderfully bogus, recalling some stockbroker's Rural Retreat, with a bricked fireplace and logs stacked as if in preparation for a Yule blaze. Here I could sit with plenty of time to look about me, for the little dining-room was full and the diners, all Spanish, tended to linger with sublime unconcern for the waiting-list: while two waitresses of the formidable race of jovial, middle-aged Spanish women came tearing in from time to time to keep my spirits up with reports of their progress and to puff their grilled trout, which was the speciality of the house.

The only other occupants of the foyer were two Americans, one an old lady with white baby curls rinsed blue, a row of expensive bracelets on her wrinkled arm and a face lifted so often that its smooth dead surface seemed to have no kinship with the neck below it at all, and the other a tired man, much younger, with sparse hair sleeked carefully backwards. She was consulting a pile of ancient tourist leaflets lyrically setting forth the glories of Spain, and now raised her head to remark: "I've been reading about this place Burgos. I sure want to see this Cathedral."

"Why," said the man, "you saw the Cathedral at Burgos."

"For land's sakes! Have I been to Burgos?"

"You certainly have."

"And did I see that Cathedral?"

"You sure did."

"Well!" she exclaimed, with a chuckle. "How do you like that?"

At last the waitress came to fetch me to dinner, but with hanging head and dragging feet, for the grilled trout were all gone.

In the morning I hired a taxi at frightful expense and drove to the Lago. The scene deserved all that was said about it: a great expanse of water, clear green and mirror-smooth save where now and again a breeze fretted the surface, enclosed by mountains with fields of pale gold corn all over their lower reaches. I have never seen an inland lake of greater beauty in Switzerland or Yugoslavia or anywhere else; and except for a girl washing clothes at the edge of it it was quite deserted. No bathing cabins, refreshment stalls or boats for hire, and not a soul in sight: and, better than that, not a sound to be heard but the girl chanting a melancholy little tune to herself or the ripple of a leaping fish. After the eternal brouhaha of Spanish life, this lovely peace was far more than the mere absence of bustle and commotion, and I lay on a rock in the sun almost drunk with it, fervently blessing the tourist officials for their lack of enterprise. Presently I went to swim: the water was warm and not icy-cold as described in the literature, but no doubt the author of this, for want of conveyance, had been unable to make a personal verification. As the morning wore on one or two motor cars drove up and by lunchtime there were about fifteen people on the sand, among them some enchanting little brown baby boys, each with his peaked cap to protect him from the sun and not a stitch of anything else: with whom their papas constantly played as if they were dolls, unable to leave them alone for a minute and fussing over them a great deal more than the mothers.

There was said to be a restaurant a mile or so from the *playa* and I set off to look for it. Like the Lago, it was in no hurry to draw attention to itself, for it was necessary to turn off down a twisting lane, unmarked and found only after repeated inquiries, and then climb down a rocky footpath almost to the water's edge before coming on it hidden among some trees. Peasants were returning home to their midday meal and rest, with scythes in their hands, their faces all cast in the same wild mould as if members of one extraordinary family: and once a group of old women dressed in black hurried past like a confraternity of witches, waving pitchforks and shrieking at the tops of their lungs. Some men were mounted on the patient burros with their swift, ladylike tread: one in particular, a huge man with a wooden leg, who rode a tiny beast that appeared to be half his size, shouted to another huge man as he went by; and this other man took a run and vaulted on to the little creature's back behind, while the burro reeled and struggled gamely on.

The people at the inn had all the reluctance of their kind to lay their cards on the table. They agreed doubtfully that it was an inn and, on being pressed, that it would be possible to have some food there. But they said, brightening wonderfully, it would not be ready for ages; and I sat for an hour and a half by the lake watching the plump trout lazily float by and the little water snakes wriggle fiercely to and fro as if wholly given up to some frantic, secret purpose. Here were strange butterflies, with black and fawn markings on white, orange flecks on lime-green wing, and the grass was gay with purple clover and meadow daisies to give a sense of home; and the time went pleasantly enough even if by now I was weak with hunger.

After the terrible and so deliberately prepared lunch had been eaten, the taxi-man appeared to announce that we must leave immediately. As no hour had been specified for our returning I was rather taken aback, but the man went on to say that with my *permiso* he should like to give someone a lift and this someone had an urgent appointment. Clearly it was all arranged, *permiso* or not, and "someone" proved to be two large men and two little boys. But in Spain when a rich foreigner hires a taxi it is naturally and properly regarded as public transport; and we all piled in, the extra bodies courteously trying not to breathe in order to cause no more inconvenience than was inevitable.

15

AT SIX on the following morning I rose to catch the bus to Vigo, which turned out to be a venerable bone-shaker just like that on the Mérida-Trujillo run: there is a fine want of consistency about the Spanish services which greatly extends the variety of experience. A bagpiper came to play us off, squealing round and round the vehicle like a terrified pig while the travellers, who, like most peasants, were already conversing at the tops of their voices, raised these further to a deafening roar. The coach bounced away up a road that wound through mountains capped with heather: in the hedges were foxglove, wild rose and honeysuckle. At the spa of Allariz it stopped in a most capricious manner and hurled everybody out, to drag their luggage half across the town to another bus for Orense, where it would be necessary to change again.

Orense was the first Galician town I saw, a dull, ugly, newish place with inhabitants to match: a reminder that Spain was left behind came almost at once, for the youth who carried my traps to the other coach complained loudly of his tip. It was twice the normal amount and his mouth was open to heckle before he had fairly counted it; but he followed me whining as I went to look for a restaurant and asserting the likes of me made it impossible for poor boys to live. Presently, seeing his laments had no effect, he changed his tune and effusively offered to show me the best eating-house in the town; and for this he had to be paid again. The money was well laid out, however, for at the table next to mine the most magnificently impulsive game of chess I have ever seen was being played: one gloriously lunatic move followed another and the board was cleared of men both black and white in a time that must have established a world record.

The Vigo coach was a monster with a Diesel engine and a sort of cockpit for the driver, where he was joined by friends as fat as himself, so that four stout men were squeezed into the space intended for one and the driver had difficulty in managing the wheel. The young man beside me crossed himself devoutly as the engine started before settling down to a pile of crude Spanish comics; and well might he do so, for the coach thundered along the twisty road like a runaway, honking at corners without slackening speed and clearly of the opinion that what happened to carts, pedestrians or frailer vehicles was altogether their own business. More and more people boarded as we went along until the aisle was stiff with them, banging heads with their parcels or simply resting an arm on top, jostling and nudging with that remarkable physical indiscretion of Spaniards which they do not in the least resent themselves or even, probably, notice. What could be glimpsed of the country through the mass of swaying bodies appeared beautiful, somewhat like the western highlands with the heather and the fir trees and the hazy northern atmosphere. And as we came near Vigo and saw the gabled houses, green or red and white, nestling among the foliage on the surrounding hills, we seemed rather to be in Carinthia or Slovenia. Charming as the landscape was, nobility had gone from it, as it seemed to have gone from the people: the nobility which is the core and essence of Spain and which you breathe in, through all the wretchedness, like invigorating puffs of mountain air.

Certainly, another race of men lived here: "exhausted and

suspicious," Ortega y Gasset calls them. At the coach terminus an old Castilian gentleman who had just landed at Vigo from Buenos Aires was engaged in a lively debate with his porter. The Gallego had carried two light suitcases for a matter of fifty yards, and now affirmed that the normal rate of pay for this exacting work was twenty-five pesetas. He was in a strong position, as the Castilian had handed him a note for this amount, and he carried his point by simply refusing to give any change. In all the years I have travelled in Spain I never saw anything of the kind before: it may seem a little thing, but Spanish honesty is so fine and, in view of the country's poverty, so moving that this Neapolitan behaviour made a nasty impression. At last the poor Castilian shrugged and gave in, smiling, rueful and more than a little contemptuous, which the Gallego, again un-Spanish, either failed to notice or did not mind.

Smiling complacently, he tucked the note away and seized my own luggage. Having warned him that I would not put up with any little comedies, I told him to bring me to a clean, modest hotel on the waterfront; and, saying with enthusiasm that he knew just the thing, he set off at a smart trot down the mean, dishevelled streets of the port. The place of his choice turned out to be most peculiar indeed and presided over by a "Madame" with curls nodding roguishly above her experienced face, a flowery silk dress and her two plump feet forced into tiny, high-heeled shoes. Assuming from my appearance and luggage that I had no money, she waved her arms and declared that all the rooms were taken; but the glance, as of forked lightning, that she shot at my wallet as I opened it to pay the man must have steadied her and, with throaty chuckles, she beckoned to me to go inside. She opened the door on a remarkably squalid room with no ventilation, for which the price marked on the wall was twenty-five pesetas a day and which, she told me, "as I was only one," I could have for fifty. While I puzzled over the logic of this she ran nimbly downstairs again and presently could be heard in passionate give-and-take with the porter, who claimed a reward for his offices in the matter. A waiter in a grimy white jacket came to ask if I were dining and, lingering coyly, invited me to go with him—or rather, perhaps, himself to go with me—to the French Circus that evening; but I declined the little treat.

"How do you know you wouldn't like it?" he asked. "You haven't really looked at me yet!"

I favoured him with a closer examination, but the answer still was no.

From the waterfront looking out through the palm trees at the blue sea with the pointed green mountains enclosing the bay Vigo makes an impression of great beauty; although it is hazardous to sit there and enjoy it, as ever and anon a small train runs shrieking along the line before it and covering everybody with greasy black smuts. But from the sea it appears a dowdy mass of grey, boxlike dwellings falling over the slopes like spilled bricks. It is without distinction of any kind, an unkempt featureless town pushed up hastily to house a population that expanded swiftly in the days of the sardine fishing. Now the sardines have swum away to other waters and the people are looking about to fill their place by industry and shipbuilding, mostly of small ships for coastal work or to the Spanish territories in Africa. One notable building there is a skyscraper leaping aggressively up and visible from miles out to sea, so that passengers on the foreign liners can exclaim at it and ask what it is. This is the Casa de Previsión, or headquarters of the National Health Service, which accommodates in good Spanish style a horde of officials whose achievements so far are derisory. But the sympathetic foreigner—and most foreigners in Spain are sympathetic, since life is immensely agreeable for them—wags his head and declares that this fellow Franco certainly gets a move on.

The faces of the people in the streets are in notable contrast to those of other regions, being closed, cunning and suspicious. If you ask one of them a question, if it is only the time of day or the way to somewhere, he will often look at you sideways as if wondering what your ulterior motive can be. An acquaintance of mine, a scholar and fervent Gallego patriot, humanly anxious to put the best face on them, said they were *desconfiado:* they had been tricked and abused so often. Some doubt of this is perhaps permissible, for, as I very soon found, they themselves were as tricky as apes in the jungle and any abusing and tricking of them that took place could only have been the work of other, more gifted, Gallegos. A point in their favour is the relative freedom and independence of their women, arising perhaps from the fact that the men spend long periods at sea, leaving their wives to manage farm or business and to function as the real heads of families. These women look a vigorous lot as they stride about the streets with great burdens on their heads, a round basket crammed with loaves, a tub of fish or vegetables, carried at top speed without the support of so much as a finger and spinning a little like a lazy top; and once I saw a woman, accompanied by two strapping males, take a cloth, twist it into a pad, lay it on her head and then hoist on top of that a huge bulging suitcase, the property needless to say of one of the men.

Here too is seen the abject poverty of other regions, particularly among the people coming in to market their produce from the countryside around. It is curious that it should be so, for the distress of the rural south is often blamed on the holding of huge estates by landlords who are absent the greater part of the year in Madrid; and in Galicia the land is largely owned by peasant smallholders. There are the familiar ragged figures and emaciated faces, the dreadfully high proportion of the afflicted, the beggars that might be found anywhere in Andalusia, and the starving animals. One morning as I sat over coffee outside the Bar Compostela a maidservant dumped three boxes of garbage on the curb near by, at which a swarm of cats, mostly pregnant, appeared as if by magic and threw themselves upon it; and a miserable bootblack who had been vainly looking for customers at once went over and combed the horrid stuff to help find morsels for them to eat, a compassionate act from one unfortunate to others.

Vigo had no apparent charm to offer eye, ear or nose and I began to think the young chemist of Mérida must have been something of a mystic. Yet there I had the good fortune to meet a number of delightful individuals, chief among these being Don Vicente. He was a twinkling old gentleman of infinite good humour and toleration, notable even in this land of personal relationships for the far-flung network of his kinsmen, each placed in a highly strategic position. Did I wish to see the Naval Cadet College at Marin? Happily, a cousin of his had once been Director of it, which established a lasting connection. Was I going to the *fiesta* at Santiago de Compostela? Then he should write a card to his cousin, Don Felipe, a notable scholar and Gallego enthusiast, who would get me a good place in all the main events. I must not think of visiting Pontevedra without looking in on his cousin the Cuban Consul. And it might be pleasant eventually to return to England by sea: in which case, as he himself was Shipping Consul and further had a cousin in the principal line, nothing would be easier. Whatever I undertook in Vigo in the way of inquiry or exploration, sooner or later the path crossed that of this charming old spider: not a local event took place but he knew the reason behind it, there was hardly a soul in the place whom he did not know; and during all the time that I enjoyed his hospitality and conversation not once did he commit himself to the expression of any opinion whatever.

Furthering no doubt some complex scheme of his own, he took me to pay a courtesy call on the *Faro de Vigo*, which was the second oldest newspaper in Spain and which had celebrated

152

its centenary in 1954. The office had the singular atmosphere
of quiet desperation common to newspaper offices all over the
world, and the journalists received us with the same fraternal
welcome. Three men were there, the Editor himself, a native of
Rivero, Francisco Leal Insua, the Gallego poet, from La Coruña,
and a third from Mondoñedo; and they sang in strophe and
antistrophe the praises of their own towns and exacted a promise
that each of them should be visited. Insua was a nice fellow with
a long, shallow, melancholy face and a sharp, somewhat acid
humour; and being famished for copy like all provincial
journalists he presently announced that he must have an interview. At this Don Vicente stirred restlessly in his chair and
muttered that now we should have to call on the rival paper
too, as otherwise there would be hell to pay. He informed them
that as my Spanish was so poor he should act as interpreter,
which nettled me a little until, from his judicious editing and
amending of my statements, I divined the purpose of it. Meanwhile the Editor was busily inscribing three thick volumes of
Insua's poetry to be added to my luggage. After that the conversation became general. None of them showed a trace of the
official hostility towards England which fills the Spanish prints
with those references to our effete and decadent democracy
which sound so oddly archaic nowadays: on the contrary, they
showed a lively interest in it and, considering the distortion and
malassessment of English news in their papers, they were remarkably well-informed. Literature rather than politics attracted
them mostly, although they begged me to explain the difference
between the Conservatives and the Socialists, as they themselves
could see none. And who were these Tories that people talked
about? On the literary side they appeared unfamiliar with de-
velopments after Oscar Wilde, except that they knew the name
of Graham Greene and had studied the work of P. G. Wodehouse, who enjoys a popularity in Spain richly deserved anywhere, but none the less bewildering. They moaned about the

153

lack of funds of Spanish newspapers: bull-fighters paid liberally for favourable notices, but they were the only people who did, and it was difficult enough to scratch up a living, nor could they ever hope to be sent about the world like their English and American colleagues. Added to which, Insua put it, it was a *desgracia* to be a poet at all; but for all this croaking they were a merry trio and it was an agreeable encounter. Don Vicente chuckled contentedly as, weighed down with volumes of poetry, local guides and histories, introductions and copies on the *Faro*, we went away: exactly what was passing in his mind, of course, I never knew.

Don Vicente put me in touch with another engaging personality, with whom, however, conversation was difficult, as he spoke twice as fast as the average Spaniard, himself no mean performer, and so explosively that the words seemed to bounce from his lips like an endless succession of hard little rubber balls. He was a fervid patriot, as were all the Gallego intellectuals I met, and was engaged in the fight to save the language, which the régime was determined to suppress. No papers or official documents might be published in it, and the children had all to do their lessons in Castilian, with a dire effect on their education, as it was not their native tongue and they never heard it at home. The Government made out that this was done to discourage separatist tendencies, but "they had invented separatism just as they invented Communism," to suit their own book: the real reason for it was that they could not grasp the idea of unity with diversity and wanted to force everything into the one mould.

With his talk of the Gallego language, the Gallego people, the Gallego tradition, the Gallego soul, he seemed, like so many intellectuals of impoverished and backward lands, a man dedicated to a myth. What was it really but self-assertion in the face of more gifted and competent neighbours? Galicia, Brittany, Wales, Ireland, the pattern repeats itself over and over again in these misty outlands on the shores of the Atlantic which, as Gerald Brenan says, empties the mind of reason and fills it with bad poetry. Everything has to be inflated beyond recognition, versifiers are puffed into major poets, rascals turned into national heroes, a small local to-do into a glorious feat of arms: and in a curious abasement of the mind the customs and beliefs of ignorant and grossly superstitious folk—who do not give a "thank you" for it—are patiently and reverently collected, expounded, analyzed and, copiously annotated, are offered to the world as proof, if such is needed, that the people concerned are not as other men are.

My friend, however, was anything but a gaunt, nail-biting fanatic: he was the merriest soul alive and handy in the highest degree with a knife and fork. Indeed, it may be wondered if the pleasures of the table did not claim nearly as much of his attention as the sufferings of Galicia. He was also a man of huge, if vague, hospitality. Our second meeting was by appointment in one of the elegant cafés on the Alameda, where after a time we were joined by a tedious man of an all too familiar type. Obsequiously washing his hands he stated that he was only a *pobre periodista* who wished to put a few questions to the "illustrious" lady: after which he went on at once to a headsplitting harangue about the Celtic race until, exasperated, I inquired whether he wanted to ask me something or tell me. "Ask! ask!" he said. "I want to ask you if you believe in the Celtic race." I told him no, except as a pretext for being a nuisance, and he complained in a snarling tone of paradoxes. At this I turned to my friend and in a voice dripping with honey said that really it was time for me to go.

"Go! You can't go," he said in astonishment. "We haven't had any lunch!"

In the course of a leisurely banquet which included a number of Gallegan delicacies, such as a peculiar kind of shell-fish that looked and tasted like the claws of a hen and in less poetic lands might not have been thought comestible, he disclosed his plans for the afternoon, evening and, indeed, the night. First, we would go by tram to the little *playa* where his summer habitation was and where his wife expected us. Then we should all go to supper with one of the neighbours who was celebrating her *santo*, La Virgen de la Carmen. After that, if I were tired, I could rest a little at the villa before returning to Vigo. The vitality of Spaniards is as admirable as appalling.

On reaching the tram-station of his *playa*, my friend felt in need of refreshment before he accomplished the last lap of the journey, a matter of two hundred yards, on foot. We sat down at a table under shady trees where there was a fine smell of the ocean in the air, and in no time two more poets came and sat with us. They described, for the foreigner's benefit and always with that odd complacency, some of the terrors that weighed on the minds of their people: the awful doings of witches, particularly at Coiro on the Eve of St. John, when they all met together to lay their wicked plans, or the dread night when the souls rise and march in a body, and God help the miserable wight who meets them on their way. I asked if the young people believed in all this nonsense, and, laughing, they said the young believed in nothing at all. Sometimes they lapsed into their own tongue, which has a pleasing sound, melodious and caressing and plaintive, nearer to the Portuguese than to the Castilian; and they sang songs, accompanying themselves with a rhythmic tattoo of their fists on the table.

At my friend's villa his wife came running out to welcome us and also to pass the word, which brought a gloom on the company, that the Chief of Vigo Police would come to the neighbour's *santo*. It appeared that his wife was an old friend of the hostess and there had been nothing for it but to invite him. A muttered consultation took place among the men, who seemed, whether for snobbish or political reasons, very loth to meet him. But it was decided that we could not decently draw back: nor, as it turned out, were there any real grounds for anxiety, for the hostess at once handed round a claret cup of such stunning potency as ironed out all artificial differences and induced a mood of warm, if temporary, good will. The Chief himself was a caricature of a Fascist policeman, short, immensely fat, with greasy, crinkled hair and a pale, sleepy, cunning face. He had but one party trick, which was to whistle like an engine between two fingers; but it appeared to give him great satisfaction and he repeated it throughout the evening at intervals which always grew shorter. About twenty guests were crowded up to the table and feasted for hours on every kind of delicious and indigestible viand, from chicken pies to cream cake; and afterwards there were songs and speeches and a good deal of the horseplay in which Spanish males of whatever region take so peculiar a delight. At last, tipsy to a man, we reeled away to the *fiesta*, of which I retain only a dim impression of crowds of people shrieking in the murky light cast by a few pale lamps here and there, blaring music, dancing, fireworks and frantic political discussion.

As I tottered into my hotel at about nine o'clock next morning, Madame, seated on a chair outside with her bosom pushed up under her chin like a pouter pigeon's, shot me a look from her lizard eyes as one girl to another and, with her fruity chuckle, remarked, "*Hola!*"

Hardly had I washed and changed than from a window I noted Don Vicente's white Panama hat moving steadily up the boulevard and hopping up and down on his head as every two minutes he passed a cousin. It had become clear that my respectable acquaintances preferred to enter the hotel no more than they must—indeed, a member of the British community had taken me aside and explained the matter with such tact and delicacy as to leave me in some doubt of what he meant—and I ran down to meet him outside. He had arranged a visit to the naval college at Marin for that afternoon, and said we might as well take in Pontevedra while we were about it. He had this way of secretly drawing up huge programs and announcing them in the most nonchalant way in the world. But, he said, he must have his siesta beforehand, for he was an old man and to do without it would certainly finish him.

The naval college was an impressive establishment indeed and beautifully placed in gardens that rose in terraces and looked over the Bay of Marin. It accommodated three hundred naval cadets for a course of five years and had splendid classrooms, living quarters, hospital and gymnasium, all spotlessly clean, modern and in good taste and with the atmosphere of quiet efficiency that seems peculiar to men of the sea in whatever country. Again and again at religious or civic processions in Spain I have wondered at the smartness of dress and drill of the naval units as compared with the military, in which no one appears to be wearing a uniform intended for him and all amble along in their own sweet time: it is odd that the two services should have such different traditions and, in a country so jealous, that one should not try to compete with the other. This school at Marin might have been a first-class naval establishment anywhere: it was the most un-Spanish concern I ever saw in my life. A young officer of Marines in snow-white uniform conducted us round the building: he was fair-haired with steady grey eyes and quiet manners, speaking excellent English, and, only that just as we were leaving he plucked a sprig of oleander and handed it to me with Latin grace, might well have been an Englishman.

Meanwhile, Don Vicente was bursting with pride, and he told me happily that the place had cost millions and millions of pesetas.

We then went to Pontevedra, the capital of the province, which had many fine old buildings and public parks and an air of leisurely dignity that was a welcome change from the graceless bustel of Vigo. The museum was notable, being richly stocked and beautifully kept, and presided over by one of those singleminded enthusiasts who appear so eccentric among their indifferent fellow citizens and yet are so typical of the Spanish provinces. It was surprising to find in this out-of-the-way corner a fine Morales, a Zurbaran and a Ribera on loan from the Prado in Madrid: or rather it seemed surprising until Don Vicente explained that the Director of the Prado was a Gallego and the Vice-Director from Pontevedra itself. Other landmarks we saw were the house where Don Vicente was born and the Church of Santa Maria, where he was baptized; and the thought of that little bundle of future know-how, disillusion and perennial devotion to the ladies in its frilly white robes, helpless what time the sponsors rejected world and flesh on its behalf, was a beautiful one. In the house of his birth now lived a cousin, the Vice-Consul of Cuba, a huge jovial man with a tremendous voice who immediately burst into a denunciation of the town and its people while his secretary stood beside him and feebly protested. Lazy, envious and full of malice! And donkeys every one. Never a tap of work, and look at him, a slave, chained to his desk. No time to shoot—and he flung out a hand at the rows and rows of silver trophies that lined the room—and look at his great pot-belly: no time even for a game of tennis to keep it down. Grind, grind, grind. I wondered what the feverish intercourse between Cuba and Pontevedra could be that so cruelly limited his natural employments, and think he may rather have overstated it, as he went on directly to invite us both to his house for a fortnight, when we should really see some sport.

But by now we had covered many long miles and Don Vicente, with further references to his age, said we should make our way home. For all that, he seemed as fresh as a daisy and I had difficulty in keeping up with him; and at the station he mumbled a crusty ham sandwich with a speed and alacrity remarkable in a man who possessed not a tooth of his own and through some prejudice or whim chose not to have any supplied.

One of the most entertaining of local characters was Mr. Mann, an English businessman who had spent twenty years in the country and was affectionately known as Her Majesty's Ambassador to Galicia. There was not a place of interest, however slight, in the whole province that he had not visited, often on foot with a knapsack on his back, to the great amusement of the people, who never walk a yard unless they must or to show off their finery. English to the core—he disclosed that *The Wind in the Willows* was his favourite reading—he had the passion for an alien culture poles apart from his own that so often is found in this romantic race: as firmly Protestant in his way as Ford, he indulged in none of the latter's ferocious witticisms at the expense of Holy Church. Considering how much he knew about her little ways, he was remarkably sympathetic: he did, indeed, express a mild astonishment at the hairrising anticlerical jokes of his Spanish friends, who he knew would be hurrying off to Mass first thing in the morning, but this has puzzled many a Protestant before, the capacity for making distinctions being an essentially Catholic one. But he showed a fine understanding in other matters that profoundly shock Protestant feelings as a rule; as, for instance, in the case of a certain unhappy priest, unable to bear the loneliness of a tiny rural parish, who had taken to the bottle and was frequently *hors de combat*.

He introduced me to the tiny fish-restaurants that are a feature of Vigo, where foreigners seldom go, where the food is served on homely checked tablecloths and the wine in earthen pots and the bill is less than half the amount in other places. The gayest and busiest of them was ruled by a formidable matriarch with heavy purple cheeks and a long black moustache, whose two grown sons had more than once run off on her account but always been remorselessly haled back; and watching her as she grimly distributed spider crab and sardine, lobster and *bacalao*, and listening to her mighty voice as she exhorted the toilers at the kitchen fire, one wondered how they ever dared attempt it.

All this pleasant hospitality Mr. Mann would attribute to mere selfishness on his part, saying that he wanted to talk about Spain; and this he would do, nineteen to the dozen, his blue eyes blazing with enthusiasm. He had much of the kind of information which, grievous to say, is more inclined to lodge in my head than weightier matters can hope to: that the statue of the Virgin in the Cathedral at Mondoñedo had started life in St. Paul's and only after many vicissitudes had reached Rivero, from whose parish she had been wrested by the Bishop and brought to her present abode, where she was known as *"La Inglesa"* and, as foreigners are apt to be, much esteemed by the faithful: that in 1687 the English Consul at Ribadeo built a lavatory which discharged itself on the roof of the Town Hall below his house, leading to a discussion in the Courts that dragged on for years: that the Spaniards in their implacable jealousy of the Holy See (*Catolicas, si! Vaticanistas, no!*) would only recognize as pilgrims those who had been to Santiago, those visiting Rome being merely *Romeros:* as well as strings of books that had to be read and of places that must be seen, which would have fully occupied my time for a couple of years at least.

Devoted as he was to the region and its people, he had never been taken in by the Celtric legend, about which he was extremely funny, offering to lend me a book with the promising and suggestive title *Six Thousand Years of Gaelic Grandeur—Unearthed: the Most Ancient and Truthful Chronicles of the Gael.* He warned me to be extremely careful in dealings with the literary world, as they would think nothing of twisting every word to suit themselves, and the ordinarily polite remarks of a visiting foreigner might well emerge from their pens as impassioned Gallegan propaganda. Of this I had an inkling, having read with amazement in a certain paper of the parallel I was supposed to have drawn between Celtic Galicia and Celtic

161

Ireland: whereas, the few if indeed striking resemblances I had noted between the two countries being such as a visitor would hesitate to mention, I had told them that I could see none. The *Faro*, however, had conducted itself in the more conservative tradition of the Press and had reproduced Don Vicente's remarks with entire fidelity.

A few days remained before the grand *fiesta* would open at Santiago, and I spent them well and lazily on the different *playas* within reach of the town, all quiet and undeveloped places where one could lie and bake in peace. On the anniversary of Franco's crossing to Spain, a national holiday called for some reason *Exaltación del Trabajo*, I went to Rodeiro, a lovely sweep of sand across the bay reached by a grunting little ferry, with a young woman who was a model in Vigo's leading fashion house. She was a native of Madrid, and much out of her element among the Gallegos, of whom she had many caustic things to say, and her description of her living arrangements was curious and diverting. Although she was over thirty and independent, the *dueña* expected her in by ten thirty every night—and ten thirty in Spain is the time when most people begin to think of dinner—and once when she had gone to a cinema with a male friend she had been warned to alter her way of life or look for other accommodation. In the early days of our acquaintance I had asked her to dine at my hotel, at the bare mention of whose name she closed her eyes with a shudder: we had to go out to a staid restaurant and eat at the fantastic hour of nine, after which I conducted her home to allay any base suspicions on the *dueña*'s part. The excellent woman was already on sentry-go at the door, raking the street with the searching, travelling eye of a lighthouse.

On the present occasion my friend had insisted on providing our lunch, and before my astonished eyes she unpacked a full Spanish meal—omelet, veal cutlets, rice croquettes, salad and a bewildering variety of sweetmeats, all bought out of her little wage and prepared in her free time: after which, having changed into an elegant sunsuit, she busied herself in erecting a tent to insure that the sun should visit no corner of her person.

That evening *The Highland Princess* put in, homeward bound from Buenos Aires, and the secretary of the British Consulate, enterprising like all New Zealanders, proposed that we crash our way on board. The first sight, inevitably, that greeted us was Don Vicente, deep in conference with the Purser. Next we went to the main lounge, which was full of Britons drinking gin. An eerie hush, an unnatural stillness hung over the room: now and again a Briton would call a steward and whisper an order in his ear as if ashamed of it: these furtive mumbles and the crackle of newspapers were the only sounds to be heard. I grew uneasy, fearing that some national disaster, grave news, perhaps, of Her Majesty, had intervened and that the Spanish papers had omitted to mention it; but there was nothing of the kind. Simply, after two months in Spain, I had quite forgotten how Britons behave.

16

BY THE TIME we arrived in Santiago de Compostela on the 24th of July night had fallen and there was nothing to be seen but the shadowy forms of low hills surrounding the city. The air was wonderfully cool and a gentle, persistent rain was falling, so that we hardly seemed to be in Spain at all. Yet very soon she gave me an impish reminder that I was. For once I had booked a room well in advance and given the address to friends at home, so that the accumulated correspondence of two months awaited me. I carried the great bundle up to my bedroom, but did not begin to open it at once. The occasion was too solemn for haste. With the grave ritual of a voluptuary I unpacked, had my bath and got into bed and only then, reclining on the pillows, reached for the first envelope with hands that trembled with eagerness: at which, as if it had been a prearranged signal, the lights went out all over the town, and did not come on again until I was asleep.

It was still raining when morning came and the old grey city, nestling among the green slopes covered with oak and pine, wore an un-Spanish look. Wild flowers of a northern blue sprouted from cracks in ancient walls and the contours of the Cathedral, church and Palace were softened by trails of weeping mist. But here was said to be the burial-ground of the Apostle James, *Padrón de las Españas*, who has given his name to cities all over the Spanish world. Rome might come it with her St. Peter, but there was a shot or two in Santiago's locker as well. The national colours of crimson and gold flew bravely from buildings public and private, loudspeakers bellowed the *Hymn to Santiago* and the accents of every region could be heard in the crowded streets.

Pilgrims began pouring in soon after daybreak. A few came in glossy motor cars and drove to the Hostal Real, once a great Catholic hospice built by Ferdinand and Isabella and now one of the smartest hotels in Spain, furnished with every comfort the twentieth-century pilgrim might require, down to a tavern with waiters in fancy dress and a man with a concertina to play the Third Man tune. Others had travelled by coach or train or stuffed themselves and their families into tiny vehicles. Others again from the outlying villages trudged patiently in by foot, bringing with them just their food and no more. These had spent the night damply, curled up under the dripping trees of the Alameda, under the rounded arches of the lanes or in doorways and halls left open for them by kindly householders: facing, as every year, in honour of their saint hideous discomforts endured by the British but once or twice in a lifetime and then for Royalty.

By noon the main thoroughfares were a struggling, seething mass. The impediments to circulation were such as would have brought the policemen of more disciplined countries to the verge of collapse. As if motorists yelling at him for information, motorists bawling at pedestrians to get out of the way, motorists making determined efforts to enter one-way streets were not enough, the Guardia on point duty must deal with the waves of confusion spread by carts, drawn by great honey-coloured oxen, grave-eyed and imperturbable, at a pace of two miles an hour. But Spanish policemen are made of iron: trilling away on their whistles like larks, they blithely reduced chaos to reasoned anarchy in no time at all.

165

At noon a series of deafening reports sent the people hurrying to the Plaza de la Quintana outside the Cathedral. Rockets of a power usually reserved to give warning of disasters at sea were being fired from the clock-tower to announce that the *fiesta* was open. The noise was greatly relished by all except a number of little babies who slept sweetly through it in their mothers' arms. To the thin scream of Gallego bagpipes there followed the parade of the Giants, representing the various nationalities who yearly for over eleven centuries have visited the holy place. For England there was a burly John Bull with fat red cheeks, a pipe and sailor's cap, the last fellow alive, one supposed, to indulge in Romish practices, but gaily applauded by the crowd. The Gallego intellectual accompanying me, who was barely able to take his eyes off the scene, said that of course all this was meant as a treat for the children.

The year had been a Holy Year, as the feast fell on a Sunday, and because of the prodigious beano then it was rumoured that the evening display of fireworks would have to be on a frugal scale. It began very late, because the local Fascist bigwig who was to preside felt disposed to sit over his dinner and, as a self-respecting Spaniard, could hardly be expected to consider the thousands of people crushed together in the Square and waiting on his convenience. At last he appeared and for an hour and a half the Cathedral was lit by gold and silver rain, green and crimson stars, illuminated crosses, huge flying lanterns that dropped blue burning oil onto the heads of the people below and rockets that went hissing up into the clouds like fiery serpents, while clouds of smoke recalling London in the worst days of the war drifted across the open space and again one's poor Nordic head spun with the uproar. It was a magnificent spectacle, but better still was the lovely baroque façade of the Obradoiro, rising so easily and beautifully from the Romanesque foundation, the delicate towers reaching up towards heaven like

166

spikes of flowers and flooded for the great occasion in a gentle, mysterious light.

It was long after midnight when the fireworks ended, but the people at once streamed off to the Fair in the Paseo de la Herradura, where the stalls and peep-shows, the fortune-tellers and bagpipe-players, the sizzling doughnuts and local wine engrossed them till the sky grew pale again over the eastern hills. Not a moment's pleasure must be lost; the orange has to be squeezed to the last drop: life is hard, the year is long and Santiago's day comes round but slowly.

After the rigours of the night morning saw them, fresh as paint, throng the Cathedral for the Solemn High Mass which is the culminating point of the *fiesta*. It was a gorgeous and protracted ceremony. At the high altar, where in dazzling light the Apostle sat enthroned, were the Archbishop and the Canons, mitred like bishops themselves, as here their privilege is, dressed in crimson and gold, and the Knights of Santiago in their long white robes with the red cross and the square white hats. On the two benches facing inwards to the long approach to the altar sat the Army in a blaze of medals, swords, gold and purple sashes and plumed helmets and the Falange, never to be outdone, in their gold and white; while from a gallery high above the nave peeped and nodded the white-winged caps of nuns as they scrutinized and discussed the assembly. The robing of the Archbishop took up a good deal of time, as, either from etiquette or sheer helplessness, he gave no assistance whatever; and then he had to receive the silver shell in which the town's offering to St. James was formerly given, but which today is a mere symbol, the grant of the secular power being made in a more prosaic fashion. It was brought to him by the Civil Governor, who delivered with it a tedious harangue with a highly political flavour; and his courteous reply, purely religious in tone, had the air of a snub. Then the great folk set out in procession to bring in the head of the martyred Apostle, and in their absence the *Botafumeiro*, or giant censer, was lashed to an immense cable by ropes and swung from one side of the Cathedral to the other. Five young men in red robes stood and pulled, each time with greater force, until at last the silver monster, with flames shooting from it, swung up to the very roof and down with a terrifying sweep to the other side, narrowly clearing the heads of the faithful in its path. Through the kindness of Don Vicente's cousin, I had been given a place immediately under it and when at last it came to a stop I found myself trembling and sweating like a frightened animal. Now the great ones solemnly returned, bearing the head: from a gallery the young novices of choristers broke out; and the Sacrifice of the Mass began. In the shadowy background of the Cathedral, meanwhile, the common folk were huddled in their thousands—workmen, tourists, old peasant women in their black shawls, old men with faces seemingly carved from wood— gazing at the brilliant spectacle in awe.

When it was over at last the bigwigs proceeded to their official banquets and the lowly streamed off to the fair again, to feast on boiled octopus dressed with oil and red pepper. This is the traditional food of the day, and it tastes surprisingly good if the octopus has been boiled enough. As the day wore on the crowds gradually thinned as the people set out for home and by evening Santiago de Compostela showed a workaday face again. Barely a sound could be heard but the perpetual dropping of the rain.

Everyday life, however, is more interesting than the most extravagant of *fiestas;* and in the days that followed I benefited by the advice and delightful company of Don Vicente's cousin, Don Felipe Cordero Carrete. He was deeply learned in all that concerned Galicia, being Secretary of the Instituto Padre Sarmiento de Estudios Gallegos, and quite wrapped up in his antiquities. For the great Cathedral itself he had a veritable passion: indeed, the only time I ever knew him shaken out of his imperturbable good humour was when he saw a youth in the precincts wearing shorts that struck him as indecent. He at once called a sacristan to have the wretch driven forth: the sacristan inclined to the view that the offender was a mere *muchacho;* and a somewhat technical discussion took place between them as to what could or could not properly be called a *muchacho*, left hanging in the air at last by the youth wandering away of his own accord.

Although the city wears a mediaeval aspect, the better residential quarters of it were built in the eighteenth century, and many fine old houses bear the *escudos* of distinguished Gallegan families. Don Felipe said it was because at that time the gentry, who had previously lived in the country and managed their own estates, for some reason had as a class decided to move to Santiago and savour the pleasures of urban life. These taking hold of them, they had later moved on to Madrid, where, needing more and more money in that gay city, they began to sell this piece of land and that until Galicia became the country of small holdings that it is today. To draw him out, I remarked that the Gallegos seemed to have a very healthy opinion of themselves and he replied with a twinkle, "We have!" The conceit was a defensive reaction because the people used to go to Madrid to find work and, being mostly illiterate, ended up as porters and night watchmen and the like; and this together with their funny accent—had I noticed, by the way, that a Gallegan accent was always good for a laugh in a Spanish theatre?—made them stock comic characters. Therefore they magnified and boasted of every little Gallegan achievement, while at the same time they were ashamed and glad to pass themselves off as something else. An example of this was La Belle Otero, who began life as a pigherd in Padrón, an hour's journey away on the coast, and then came to Santiago as a fruitseller, where a poet fell in love with her. After this she never looked back and throughout her gay career had always pretended to be Andalusian: only now, verging on ninety, would she own to the damaging truth.

His explanation sounded as reasonable as familiar, and in refreshing contrast to the brays of the Celtic fraternity. Like all the true intellectuals of the region which I was to meet, Don Felipe was as frank as could be: indeed, in point of view and in manners they were so distinct from the body of the people as to seem of a different race, which was a great change from the aristocratic south.

Indefatigably he conducted me to every place of note within the boundaries and suggested a number of expeditions to the country round about; and yet my greatest pleasure was to amble through the streets and look at the people. The women here dashed along with even more staggering loads on their heads than in Vigo: they made nothing of a milk-can or so, or a sack of potatoes, and would often be clasping a pig in their arms at the same time. Don Felipe said it astonished even him, used as he was to it, and he told me that the fisherwomen of Marin used to carry huge baskets of fish on their heads to the market at Pontevedra, seven miles away, every morning; and they used to do it at a run, as the first women in would get the best prices for the fish.

The clergy were an interesting study as well. Never but in Rome have I seen so rich an assortment: the ground was black with them. Those of the Cathedral might be divided roughly into two sorts, the fat and the thin. The fat, which predominated, could be subdivided into the jovial-fat and the cynical-fat, while the thin were pale, nervous, intense, often hawk-nosed and with a general air of believing that the abolition of the Holy Office was a grave mistake. They wore splendid flowing capes which danced round them in billowing folds, so that ascending and descending the steps before the Cathedral on a windy day they looked like some clerical *corps de ballet;* and when they passed each other in the street they swept off their beavers with a flourish. Then there were the *Curitas* from the country par-

170

ishes, humble and admiring in their shabby soutanes, clutching umbrellas and gazing openmouthed at the magnificent churches. Now and again a fat, pink Bishop from France would pass in his motor, puffing contentedly at a cigar; and there were hosts of priestlings or seminarists, with famine in their boyish faces, the pride of their families and immensely self-conscious. At every corner you brushed shoulders with holiness and my hotel rejoiced in the presence of a Bishop under its very roof: a mixed blessing, for as soon as he entered the dining-room we must all leap up with a dreadful alacrity and mumble responses to a long-drawn-out grace of his choosing, while our food, never hot, grew steadily cooler.

It was thanks to their deplorable zeal that there was so little entertainment in Santiago. Apart from the cinema, there was only a mild cabaret at the Hostal, and this the Archbishop ordered to close at eleven, the time when theatres in Spain usually open, on the ground that the students would spend their time in it instead of working. In fact, of course, students could never afford such a treat: and they were discouraged from healthy and innocent recreation, such as dancing, for fear they fall into sin. Brothels were another matter, and these the clergy tolerated as a *malo menor* to save Pure Woman from Bestial Man: although they could not be allowed, in the city of the Apostle, to function openly and a stranger anxious to visit one had to mutter the fact into a cabman's ear.

There was huge delight therefore when the Lope de Vega company arrived from Madrid to present the great hit of the year, *La Muralla*. Over a thousand performances had been given in the capital and the printed text had run into ten editions in seven months. It was, we were told, a great vital Catholic work, challenging and pricking the conscience of Spain: a country priest had written to the author saying, "You have done more on your stage than ever I in my pulpit," for which he was rewarded with the dedication: the manuscript had been submitted to various prominent Churchmen lest it contain any error.

What these learned and estimable gentlemen could have been thinking of, it is hard to imagine. The hero, living comfortably in Madrid on the income of an estate in Badajoz, has a heart attack and senses that his last days are approaching. Only now, in the face of death, does he feel some remorse for the fact that the estate was not willed to him at all but to another, a Red and a good-for-nothing, always in and out of jail. The hero had possessed himself of it by means of a trick in the confusion following the Civil War, and the lawyer who managed the business for him is dead. From an earthly point of view there is no need for anxiety, but he worries about his chances in Heaven. He believes he must restore the estate to the owner, and a priest (speaking in a Gallegan accent which, sure enough, brought down the house) agreed. It means reducing his family to poverty and ending the engagement of his daughter to a rich young man; and when he breaks the news to them he runs up against the *Muralla*, the wall of family opposition. Although his wife is a good, devout, Mass-every-morning Spanish lady, she has no sympathy with his plan whatever. The author's solution to the impasse was quite the epitome of bourgeois cynicism: his hero is carried off by another heart attack and, dying in the resolve to do right, will presumably go to Heaven: while his family, since he has not been able to make the arrangements, continue to enjoy the property. The theatre was crammed with people, many of them in Holy Orders, who cheered this odd little piece to the echo; and while the local critics adopted a rather superior and denigratory tone, as befitted provincials dealing with a success from Madrid, not one had apparently noticed that it was not a Catholic play at all.

Having missed a good deal of the dialogue, I bought a copy of the book, afterwards presenting it to Don Felipe, who sat over it with a long face and dejectedly shook his head.

He was particularly anxious that I should pay a visit to the *pazo* of Oca, a country house of the early eighteenth century lying about twenty kilometers from Santiago; and accordingly I rose in pitch darkness to take the bus at six o'clock, reaching the little village soon after seven. Everything was shrouded in mist, drops of moisture hung in the vine leaves and the heather, and long wet cobwebs trailed from the briars in the hedge, the whole scene like a melancholy page from one of Pardo Bazan's novels. The *pazo* was a fine mellow building of grey stone, with coats of arms on the walls and an air of tranquil recollection about it as if it were turning over in its mind all that had ever taken place under its roof. At right angles to it stood the old family chapel with an iron grille for a door through which could be seen the candles of the altar, as early Mass was being said; and in front was a broad space of turf, green and smooth as an Oxford lawn. I sat on a pile of logs waiting until the caretaker could decently be roused up. A few peasant women went by on their way to the fields, wearing men's boots several sizes too large for them, and they would pause for a word or two in the frank, abrupt style of Gallegan women. All mentioned the fact that to get into the grounds would cost three pesetas, rather in the tone of one who says "a whole guinea." Presently Mass ended and the people began trickling over the lawn in twos and threes: a fine provincial assortment, old countrywomen with black shawls and black silk kerchiefs on their heads, a little girl in deep mourning, probably at Mass to pray for someone recently dead, giggling maidens and a wonderful old gentleman, very much the *señor*, with a curly spade beard, a decoration in his buttonhole and his hat on at a rakish angle, who called out, "Are you waiting for a bus? Because, you know, there isn't one," as he tripped jauntily by; and at the end the priest himself rushing home with leaping spectacles and a great swirl of black skirts to his breakfast.

An hour or two later the caretaker came. The grounds were

open to the public, but not the house, which belonged to a *duque* who, however, preferred to sizzle on his estates in Seville. There was none of the neglect so often found in such properties in Spain, where rich people seem to buy places and forget all about them: everything was trim and cared for, with shady walks and brilliant flower-beds, a long avenue of old lime trees, a pond with trout swimming to and fro and heavy bunches of blue hydrangeas reflected in the water, deliciously cool and inviting. As a treat the caretaker unlocked a door in the court-yard and led the way up stone stairs to the ducal dining-room, austere as the refectory of a convent, with a long bare table, stuffed and mounted heads of deer all down the walls and one bad painting of a seventeenth-century nobleman on horseback: all kept as clean as a whistle in readiness for the Duke who never came.

But now it was just ten o'clock and there was no bus back until the evening. I thought of returning to Santiago on foot, but the sun was warming up and I sat down on the banks of the River Ulloa instead. There was nothing to see but the efforts of two little boys who flogged and flogged the water with their fishing-rods and never caught a minnow all morning, and nothing to do but eat a small part of the meal provided by the hotel, the Spanish idea of a picnic basket being the full four courses of a set luncheon, dismally cold and wrapped in greasy paper. At about two in the afternoon I lost all patience and, walking to the nearest village, tried to hire a taxi. They had none, and appeared to find amusement in the very idea of such a thing. On, therefore, to the next, with the same result; and there was nothing for it but to sit, hot, exhausted and furious at the side of the road until the evening coach came by, the whole day gone in visiting a place roughly as far away as Hatfield House from Marble Arch.

Another expedition was to Padrón, passing Esclavitud, so named because a man, miraculously healed there by water from the Virgin's spring, at once gave her his cart and two oxen for saving him from the "slavery of sickness"; Padrón is the place where the vessel bringing the Apostle's body from Iria tied up. There is nothing much to commemorate the event except for a pretty fountain with a carving of the Apostle, his head now in its rightful place, supine in the boat with a baby angel in charge of navigation and two pilgrims keeping watch; but there are beautiful walks in the countryside around. It was a pleasure to see happy, well-fed dogs again and the cared-for oxen, with their shining yellow coats and wide, blue-tipped horns: the Gallegos cherish their beasts as partners in toil, loving them and working at their side, which is perhaps the reason why there is little enthusiasm for the *corrida* in the region. The plant life was curious in its mingling of north and south: alongside the bean-rows and cabbages in the smallholding grow vines and Indian corn, and orange or camellia trees in the little gardens, while dotted about in the fir and oak, heather and gorse of the hills are palms and eucalyptus, all doing equally well. And there are charming features peculiar to the northern *aldea*: the *orreos*, or cribs for storing grain or hay, which, raised from the ground on stone legs, look like so many Noah's Arks, with a cross at one end of the tiled roof and a second finial of either religious or superstitious import at the other: the *cruzeros*, or grey stone crosses of Galicia, with the Crucified on one side and the Virgin on the other, various figures carved on the stem and frequently skulls and bones round the pedestal; and the little ricks, beautifully rounded and trim, with a rope of hay twisted in decorative loops on the top with a twig of apples attached in a spirit frankly pagan.

There was hardly a man to be seen: the male population must either have gone to sea or to America. Everywhere in the fields were women, lifting the golden new potatoes from the brown earth or striding homeward with the great bundles on their heads. Their tongues were as active as the rest of them, and they had no objection at all to putting a foreigner in her place. Beautiful! *Padrón* beautiful? For you, not for us. We are slaves. We have to work all day, in the fields, up the mountain. And for what? Nothing at all. To have to live and die in such a place, think of it. Such remarks would be punctuated by shouts of laughter. As I listened to them there came into my mind the description of the Galician woman by Rosalia de Castro's husband in the course of his attack on the Countess Pardo Bazan: *"¿Porque siendo mujer y gallega no conoce la mujer gallega, sobre cual cae todo el trabajo y todo el dolor de su tierra?"* These bitter, laughing women did carry a load of toil and sorrow on their backs: the devotion to them of the melancholy de Castro was not to be wondered at. She herself, Spain's greatest woman poet, was of their race and spent her troubled life at their side: she knew privation and in one of her poems she speculates ironically where her funeral expenses are to come from. Now she has a statue in the gardens behind the Herradura in Santiago and a tomb in the Church of San Domingo, where Mass is said for her on the day after the Feast of St. James and the Gallego intellectuals all appear in their best clothes; and in their fields the nameless women of her country continue to labour the year round as they did when she was living.

17

SANTIAGO PRAYS, Pontevedra sleeps, Vigo works, La Coruña enjoys itself, as they say in the region; and a visit to La Coruña is an experience which no student of either the Spanish temperament or Spanish economics should miss. The city has an air of perpetual holiday: the streets are crammed with people laughing and talking, carefully dressed, and seemingly without a care in the world. There is little entertainment, nothing much in the way of architecture, an afternoon walk to the Roman lighthouse disposes of the antiquities, the beaches are few and some way off, and besides are raked by cool breezes from the Atlantic: what exactly brings the Madrileños here in their hundreds or inspires the unflagging gaiety of the local inhabitants it is hard to discern. The chief distraction is to walk slowly up and down the waterfront, dressed to kill, at noon and again in the evening; and presumably the rest of the day is spent in preparation for this. Eating and drinking occupy a good deal of their time as well, and it is pleasant to see them range along the Calle de los Olmos, a street given up to restaurants and bars, in search of the best meal. Each window has its display, of great red lobsters, roasted chicken, purple grapes, gold melons, prawns with their whiskery, indignant faces wreathed in lettuce, the huge round Gallegan pies and the lilac octopus poised in rubbery grace on its dish; and from one to another the people go,

177

peering through the glass and comparing and debating with the grave intentness of children. The characteristic smell of the street is of hot olive oil, its peculiar sound the clink of dice on marble-topped tables, a pastime in which dignified old ladies are seen to indulge with the rest and which has the power, probably unique in Spanish games, of holding the players dumb with excitement.

Here at last, it would seem, are Spanish people with plenty of money and the leisure to enjoy it. But when you have been in the place some while and consulted the more serious members of the community, you learn that this is not quite the case. Nearly everyone is spending well beyond his means: the city lives, as a banker expressed it, on *dinero ficticio*, or imaginary money. The merchants, he said, kept going with bills which they renewed time and again and which, for complicated Spanish reasons, the banks never called in; but how the people managed not only to subsist on their salaries, but even to cut a dash, he was unable to explain. It was a mystery, too, how things kept going at all.

The *dia intensiva* had recently been adopted, which meant in theory that people worked hard from eight to two and had the rest of the day to themselves, but in practice they turned up at about ten or eleven as before, merely respecting the second part of the arrangement. This informant was an eldery man who had spent all his life in La Coruña and knew a great deal about the inhabitants and their affairs. On Sundays he would often go out into the country or to a beach and come across a young blade of his acquaintance treating a girl to a beautiful spread of cake and pastry and candied fruits. All these things were very costly nowadays and he knew to a peseta what the boy was earning. Where did the money come from? And the young women with their fourteen or fifteen dresses? How did they do it? All were gaily spending money that, to his knowledge, they did not possess and had so been doing for years.

The situation was one that might have appealed to Pérez Galdós; and the beauty of it was that there was nothing hectic, feverish or unwholesome in the air, as might have been expected in such a nest of fritter-bugs: the prevailing atmosphere was one of calm, dignified enjoyment.

I fell in with another keen observer, an explosive little old gentleman with white curly moustaches and a number of diamond rings on each hand, who confirmed all the statements of the first and, going further, remarked that La Coruña was an image of the country as a whole. He too was blest if he knew how things continued at all. General Franco had enormously raised the pay of the Army and the Navy, and made great financial concessions to the Church: thus he had the three of them in his pocket ("You and I would do the same!") but where was the money to come from? The Government had just brought in a new law for income tax under which everyone had to declare what he had, as in England, but it would never work. It would never work because the men in charge of the department concerned were the last people who wanted it to. "Of course, I shouldn't be saying all this." All they had done was run up a fine new building in Madrid and stuff officials into it. (I had already been told that the Inspector for this region had a private office in La Coruña where, for a consideration, people could take their accounts to be juggled; and a very sensible and humane idea it seemed.) And what happened to the money they did collect? The people paid health insurance and employment insurance and saw nothing for it. Had I been to the country? Did I know how they lived? Well, then. But the Government stuck taxes on this or that, articles from abroad, entertainments, the dear knew what. If you had a cup of coffee after dinner in certain restaurants it was *Lujo* and you paid a tax on it. And that stamp they put on every telegram that was delivered. That really stuck in his gullet. Had I noticed the word *volontario* on it? But just let a Spaniard try refusing to pay! And you could get nothing, absolutely nothing, done without bribery. It was all very well if you had the money, but if you hadn't? Your dossier simply went to the bottom of the pile again as regularly as it came up. In Spain it was impossible to go straight. Quite impossible. Not to be attempted.

The foregoing tirade was delivered with the greatest good humour and frequently interrupted by bursts of chuckles.

"General Franco is a nice man," were the old gentleman's final words, "but he doesn't know half of what goes on."

I had heard this opinion a great many times before and wondered, if indeed the Caudillo is ignorant of all he is alleged to be, whether he were really the man for his post.

At this time La Coruña was preparing for its fiesta, which promised to be of an extravagance in keeping with local sentiment. In the *plaza* outside the town hall workmen were installing a huge and absurd model of the Roman lighthouse leaning forward to pin yet another medal on the enormous bosom of a wooden figure, whose gross red face was stretched in a foolish smirk. This rude effigy, it was explained, was of the Mayor, a gentleman noted both for obesity and for the delight he took in orders and decorations of every kind. He was guarded by four immense toy soldiers of grotesque appearance, all stuffed, like himself and the lighthouse, with fireworks. The men were using a fireman's ladder, from the very top of which one of them was screaming instructions to his mates on the ground as he perilously swayed about far above their heads: the whole scene suggested a nursery in the house of a lunatic giant, and a crowd of adult citizens watched it by the hour with the grave, unwinking silence of Moors.

In the evening the town assembled to see the fun. On one side of the *plaza* a dance band was playing, on another shrieked some *gaiteros*, or bagpipes, while from a third came the rich notes of a brass band; and couples were shuffling about on the dusty flags and in and out of the trees in a confused attempt to dance to the strains of all three. At midnight began a wonderful display of fireworks, with the usual clouds of acrid smoke and the usual little mishaps, such as rockets going astray and bursting among the people and flaming oil and debris raining down on their hair and clothes. Here and there members of the audience could be seen hastily beating out small fires that had started on their persons: one would like to know how many of the afflicted one sees in Spain are victims of a *fiesta*. Finally came the chief attraction, the burning of the mayor, with the lighthouse and soldiers. To judge by the screams of joy as the flames licked round the portly figure, he was not altogether beloved; and when the last firework had exploded in his interior and the charred skeleton crashed to earth with a glorious fountain of sparks, the people all but went off their heads. An ancient, wheezing fire engine now drove shakily up and played on the scorching flames a puny jet of water which, however, faltered and died almost at once; and an anxious cry went up for buckets and volunteers. Exhausted, I went home to my hotel, which I had picked out for its beautiful name, *La Primitiva Luz,* and in which the light was by no means the only primitive element; and the people danced on till the morning.

The next day was Sunday and I went to early Mass at the romanesque parish church of Santiago. On each side of the high altar was a statue of Our Lady, Mother of God: to drive the theological point more forcibly home, one showed her in the last uncomfortable phase of pregnancy with a hand dramatically pressed to the swollen womb, and the other daintily offering the breast to the Baby. In both she was balancing a heavy golden crown on her head, as a Gallega might balance a pail: the figures were curiously charming and innocent and funny. Afterwards I went on to San Jorge, where all the great were assembled for the Solemn High Mass of the *fiesta*. Here again no expense had been spared, for there was a full string orchestra as well as the organ, and each was going its own way to the detriment of the liturgy, while beautiful white flowers covered the high altar and pink ones carpeted the pedestal where the Virgin stood, richly dressed in white and gold. In the rear and side chapels, however, were the customary withered blooms or paper roses of Spanish churches: one must never expect too much. The occasion was interesting to me as the only one of its kind on which I have seen Spaniards openly display impatience and boredom. A fat Dominican rose in the pulpit and preached interminably a crazy nationalist sermon in which the word *España! España! España!* beat on our dazed ears with the monotony of a clock. The good man evidently believed this to be his finest hour, or couple of them; but his unlucky hearers shifted from one leg to the other, muttered, eased their collars and mopped their streaming brows. The police Guard of Honour went so far as to organize a relief rota, by which four men were allowed to retire for a smoke outside; and the look on their faces as they returned and found the chubby friar still leaping up and down in his box, wagging his head and waving his arms, was pitiful to see.

Thoughts of a lamentably secular nature came into my own head. San Jorge was the church that Doña Emilia, Condesa de Pardo Bazan, used to attend: Murguia, the historian whom Rosalia de Castro married, once made some rude remarks about her stepping down from her elegant carriage just in time for the short twelve o'clock. What would she have said to this prolix friar? Imagination boggled at it. A formidable, malicious lady she appears from her portrait, this Spanish Madame de Staël, with the narrow, wicked eyes under the leaping brows and the immense, aggressively high bosom. Once she invited the priests from the neighbouring country parishes to her table and when the poor souls sat down, licking their lips in anticipation of a square meal, proceeded to torment them with theological conundrums: such little tricks diverted her greatly. The hostility this famous, wealthy aristocrat displayed to the impoverished, unhappy Rosalia de Castro was a sad little tribute from talent to genius: too much of an artist herself to withhold admiration as a critic, she yet found a generous personal attitude beyond her power. From there arose the many futile squabbles, proving that literary life in Spain at the turn of the nineteenth century was no different from that in other places at other times; and when, poor Rosalia dead, the Countess spoke an *elogio* at the memorial session, she thought of nothing but the figure she herself was cutting and how her voice was and what her audience thought.

Lost in these reflections, I only gradually became aware of something strange in the atmosphere. It was merely that the Dominican had stopped shouting; and, the remainder of the Mass having been taken at impressive speed, the congregation rushed for the open air. I went on to look at Doña Emilia's town house in the old quarter, a good patrician building with *escudos* on its walls and which was still owned by the family. A fate worse than demolition had overtaken her country seat at Méiras, for in 1940 it was spontaneously offered to General Franco by the grateful people of La Coruña Province. The peasants, who paid their tax assessment four times in a year, in that year were required to pay it five; while business people in the city were informed how much their contribution would be. Enclosed with the individual's assessment was a form to sign and return with the money, saying that he "wished" to subscribe the sum in question. In this way money was quickly raised, not only to buy the house, but to furnish it from top to bottom, even to stocking the library, with what type of volume, however, I was unable to learn.

From the Condesa's house up to the tomb of Sir John Moore was a pleasant little walk. In this hallowed spot, however, there had to be one of those mental reorientations that so often are called for in Spain regarding historical matters, as from school-room memory I had vaguely believed the occasion to have been one of splendour and renown, and the crabbed little notice put up by the Spanish Government plainly showed that they took a different view. Apparently it had been one of those defeats, catastrophic for our friends, in which we so oddly delight; but the place was decently kept, Wolfe's poem had been politely carved on one tablet and on another a poem by Rosalia de Castro, which was in the vernacular and whose message had to remain secret.

From there I walked out to the Roman lighthouse, or Tower of Hercules, perched on the bare, grassy end of the peninsula. From the top of it was a beautiful view of the low, wooded hills encircling the port, and of the bay with the little boats tossing up and down on the water and a breeze rustling a field of ripe corn on shore. Works were in progress, as they are in every part of Spain where the eye of the foreigner may rest: in this case a long costly road was being built up to the foot of the tower itself, serving no real purpose and spoiling the look of the green slope. No expense is too great, no trouble too much, when it comes to diddling the outside world with a show of efficiency: the motto is: "Silk hats before breakfast." In a field near by a long line of peasant women were lifting potatoes, toiling in the wake of a crude harvester drawn by oxen, their wrinkled faces turned to gold by the sun.

On returning to the city I found it becoming a sort of Bedlam. The citizens were bent on extracting every last drop of enjoyment from their *fiesta* and, as in Spain there can be no pleasure without noise, they were shouting and screaming at the top of their lungs, supported from time to time by the Municipal Band as it marched through the streets or by itinerant groups of bagpipers, with now and again a thunderous report as some-body sent off a rocket. The very diners in the restaurants appeared to be using their knives and forks as percussion instruments in a mad music of their own, and the people outside the cafés conducted their conversation in a sustained roar.

On a sudden impulse, like a bolting horse, I packed and

184

caught the bus to Finisterre, whose name evoked the image of a desolate, rocky shore where the only sounds would be the cry of birds and the beat of waves. It was a long, beautiful drive through hills gay with heather and broom and fields where the crimson tufts of the Indian corn made a brave show beside the cold blue leaves of the kale. Only two small incidents occurred on the way, but each was illuminating. As we bounded along with the peculiar movement of Spanish coaches, which always suggests that they are really airplanes unsuccessfully trying to leave the ground, the mail-bag casually thrown with other packages onto the roof fell down into the road. This I notified first to the man beside me and then, failing to interest him in it, to the driver himself, who laughed and shrugged and gaily pressed on; and the little episode helped to explain, vividly and reasonably, the delays and disappointments of the Spanish postal system. And just before Corcubión a wild, scurvy, drunken fellow boarded the coach and began, in a hoarse bellow, to discuss the Civil War, reviling the Nationalists in terms of the vilest obscenity. The interesting thing here was that he sat next to a Guardia Civil, with rifle between his knees, who listened and smiled in perfect good humour and something almost like appreciation. As the man's language grew more and more purple, there came the warning "*Tsss! Tsss! Tsss!*" and the indignant "*¡Eso, no!*" of outraged public opinion until at last the conductor halted the bus and ordered him off, the representative of the State still manifesting a tranquil amusement and nothing more.

At Corcubión it was suddenly announced, in the Spanish manner, that the coach would go no further and that we must wait an hour and a half for a bus to Finisterre. I had a glass of terrible wine in the local inn and asked for *mariscos*, but was assured that the seas were too high for the men to put out and catch them. To my northern eye the seas looked very moderate indeed. The host brought a piece of stale cheese instead, and,

185

sitting down on the bench beside me and puffing a vile cigarette into my face, he urged me not to go to Finisterre, because they had no cinema there and the people were dirty and ignorant. His own inn was as dirty a place as you could hope to find.

It was after ten o'clock of the evening when the bus reached the end of the journey, where it was awaited by a gang of starveling children. These immediately flung themselves, screaming like gulls, on my luggage and fought vigorously for the privilege of carrying it to the only *fonda* in the place. The winner was a barefoot little girl of six or seven, who placed one heavy bag on her head and would have taken the other in her tiny hand if she had been allowed. We marched along the narrow, dirty street of which Finisterre mainly consists, accompanied by other children shouting insults and horrid personal comments and attracting numbers more by their din. The *fonda* was more of a shack than a house, with splintery wooden floors and rattling windows, lit by a dull yellow light which gave it the appearance of a witches' cave; and its grim, suspicious landlady suited it down to the ground. Reluctantly she agreed that there was a room and inquired, in a furious growl, if I wanted dinner. Encouraged by a glimpse of a fine rosy lobster on a sideboard and two great hams hanging beside the fire in the kitchen, I said that I did; and, still growling, she retired, to emerge in an hour's time with oily fried eggs and a piece of veal that was knotted like wood. That lobster, those hams, can only have been a stage property of some kind, for they were, three days later, unmoved. The wine of the country deserves a word or two. It looked and tasted like raspberry vinegar, but continued to make itself felt long after drinking by furring the tongue and leaving behind a pungent flavour, as the fumes of anthracite do. But the saddest thing of all was to find the great Spanish conspiracy against peace and quiet in full vigour here as well. That night, just as I was dropping off to sleep at last, a man lurched into my room and out again, apologizing in an indignant tone as if somehow I were to blame: then another went caterwauling drunkenly all the way up the long street and down it again; and this was followed in turn by an anthem from the cats on the roof which lasted till the coming of dawn.

The village of Finisterre is one of the most wretched communities I ever saw. The people depend on fishing for their livelihood and the weather at this westerly tip of the peninsula is more often than not too bad for them to go out. There will be one day of calm to four of high wind and one or two of fog. In hard times there is no public assistance for them, and when they are ill they give the doctor some fish, or, if they are killing an animal, a piece of meat: he, poor fellow, has a retainer of a thousand pesetas a month from the State and beyond that must shift for himself. The people are wild and savage, with the wrecker's mentality found in such places, and it is said they would steal the laces out of a man's boots. Many of them live in cabins unfit for pigs, so appalling that no rent is charged for them; but although fifty *viviendas* have been built in recent years only eleven applications were put in, as the people either found the seventy-five pesetas a month too much or else preferred the conditions they were used to.

There was little to do in such a place but walk, followed everywhere by the rabble of furious children. One seedy café there was, in the middle of the main street, in which no one but myself ever appeared to sit. Men would stride in and silently gulp down a glass of horrible wine at the counter, and stride out again. There was no social life of any sort. The coffee was indescribable, but I was glad of the place as a refuge, because for some reason the children would never come inside but remained in the street, their faces pressed eagerly to the window and distorted as in some nightmarish fun fair. In spite of everything the proprietress was a fervent

187

patriot and spoke of Finisterre as if its treasures were inexhaustible; and when on the day of my departure I passed her door she called out in an angry voice, "You soon had enough of us, then."

A couple of miles or so from the *pueblo* was the lighthouse, reached by a winding white road cut into the mountain so that one side of it was steep cliff with the sea foaming angrily at its foot. It was a most lavish and up-to-date establishment, with long, tiled corridors, gleaming iron stairways as on board a ship and a wonderful lamp in four sections of cut glass, like the fancy lighting in an expensive Parisian hotel, which rested on a pond of quicksilver. The young man in charge declared that it was the finest in all Europe, and he enjoyed himself a great deal by suddenly turning on the fog siren, which resembled nothing so much as the bray of twenty thousand asses and all but frightened me to death. I am no judge of a lighthouse, but this did seem to be a superlative one and to provide one answer to the eternal Spanish question of where all the money goes.

The only other thing to see, Finisterre's one little claim to importance, was the miracle-working image of Christ in the fourteenth-century *parroquia*, Santa Maria de las Arenas. I found it in a side chapel, a dejected figure with a Byzantine cast of feature and long artificial hair streaming over its shoulders, dressed in a black velvet skirt embroidered with gold. Four peasant women were chanting the rosary before it, and one of these immediately sprang up to show me round. She was unable to tell me the image's history or give any account of its miracles, but she recited the times of all the services without drawing breath and produced a collecting-box from nowhere, as if she too were gifted with supernatural powers. A tip she resolutely declined, until we agreed that it should be an offering to Our Lady of Fatima and not to herself:

only, as I was leaving the church, I saw her show the note to the other women in triumph before tucking it away in her stocking. They then continued the saying of the rosary.

Trickiness seemed to come as naturally to these simple fisherfolk as breathing. The small girl who had carried my luggage on the first evening had constituted herself a most unwelcome bodyguard and seldom if ever left my side. Having led me to a beach one afternoon for a swim, she intimated that she was not in business for her health and that a payment on account would be timely. She was given five pesetas and appeared to be well content, but twenty minutes later I came out of the water to find her the very picture of woe. Tears were streaming down her cheeks—*genuine tears*. For she had lost the money in the sand. I dug about for it vainly for half an hour and then gave her a new note in its place before going behind a boat to dress; she did not hear my footsteps as I re-emerged and sat there, contemplating the two notes with a look of rapture on her little face.

The Gallegos are never tired of impressing on the stranger that they are a race apart and have little in common with other Spaniards; and I am able to confirm that this is so.

As time went on the hostess of the *fonda* grew accustomed to me and became more friendly: she never actually smiled, but at least she no longer scowled heavily whenever I chanced to appear. Her meals kept pace with her temper, and once she served an excellent *caldo Gallego*, which is a thick soup of kale, beans and bacon greatly prized in the region. But there were fleas in the bed. This happens but rarely in Spain, and then must be endured in silence, as the invariable answer to a complaint is that you brought them with you. Further, I had to sleep with all the windows shut, as otherwise battalions of hungry cats leaped in and out all night. And added to all this was the infernal screaming of the children as they hunted me implacably through the streets. I began to pine for the relative tranquillity of La Coruña on *fiesta* night: the silent shores of Finisterre had been just another romantic dream, and after three nights of misery I packed and fled.

18

IN ALL GALICIA one of the most diverting, if melancholy, places to visit is Mondoñedo, lost in the wilds of the province of Lugo. The journey to it was terrible, fraught with such rigours that the clerk at the booking station tried to persuade me not to go: the road was the worst in the country, he said, and there was nothing to see in the end. As for the trains, he would not speak of them, but conveyed his opinion by laughing like a madman.

There was, then, the normal rising at the cold, misty hour of five for the morning coach, which arrived at Lugo city at ten and tossed everyone out there to wait until four for an evening one to Mondoñedo. It was cruel, for Lugo was as hot as a furnace and as dull as could be. In the Oficina de Turismo were the usual paranoiac leaflets, claiming among much else "an impalpable spirituality mounting up the belfries and soaring to the sky by the tops of her privileged Cathedral." It is strange how people fall back on impalpable excellences when the tangible ones are missing. In the English version of the leaflet the Celtic fiend had been at work: "Possibly Celtic folks chose the woods of this country as their religious and poetic center, erecting sacred monuments to their deity 'lug'." But the Spanish said austerely and factually that it had been a Roman *castro* by the name of Lucus Augusti.

191

Weary of trailing from one impalpable spirituality to another, I sat in the gardens with a Spanish translation of a tale by P. G. Wodehouse. Without a motor car of one's own in Spain one can spend whole days in waiting for conveyances to take one somewhere just a few miles off. And my efforts to spin out the luncheon interval came to nothing, for the serving of meals is the one thing in this leisurely land that is done in a hurry. The second course is placed on the table to cool before one is fairly into the first, and no sooner does one get to work on it than the waiter comes panting up to know what shall follow. But the time went slowly by and at last we all climbed into the bus for another three hours of jolting and banging and sweating.

Mondoñedo had a curious, pensive charm that made itself felt from the minute of arrival. The country round about was savage and mountainous, the lower hills being covered with trees and purple heather: twilight was falling now and an early autumnal mist went creeping up the slopes in cold white tongues. Bonfires twinkled all over the valley in fields where the peasants were still at work. The town itself seemed entirely given up to dozing and remembering. The Alameda de los Remedios would have been a perfect setting for some melancholy tale of Spanish provincial life, with the trunks of trees looming up in ghostly fashion through the mist, the blur of pale lights here and there, the couples enlaced on the wooden benches, a group of skirted priests talking in low voices, a man singing a plaintive Gallegan song. There was a feel of soft decay in the air. One could imagine a Spanish Bovary pacing angrily up and down under the moist branches in the avenue, or importuning the Virgin—miraculous also here, as she would have to be—in the Church of Nuestra Señora de los Remedios near by. It seemed no place for anyone under seventy.

Soon after ten o'clock the next morning, I called on the *cronista* of the town, Don Eduardo Lance-Santar, a scholar, author and impassioned antiquarian, noted for eccentricity among even the eccentrics of the region. He lived in a tiny, narrow house in a mean little street, with a half-door opening on to a hall in which was a second door, firmly bolted, leading to the stairway; and in this was a peep-hole, so that he could never be taken by surprise. The windows of the first floor were shut and barred, those of the second flung wide open, so that it might be assumed he was up and about; or, at any rate, still alive. There was, however, no reply to my knock and, encouraged by shouts and laughter from the shopkeepers over the way, I knocked again more loudly. Yet nothing happened, and I followed the good old Spanish custom of going away for an hour and a half. Then I came back and knocked again. Now at last one of the lower windows was pushed up and there slowly came into view the head and shoulders of a frail old gentleman, dressed in what seemed to be a night-shirt, with a bony skull and an aquiline nose, and an enormously extravagant beard, white and silky at the top and falling away into yellow curls towards the solar plexus. It was a beard to remember as long as life. Politely its owner asked me to come back in an hour: he should wish to show me the Cathedral, and Masses for the day would continue until then. When the hour had passed, Don Eduardo shuffled downstairs and emerged blinking into the open, now wearing a good grey suit, with his beard nicely combed and waving a little in the breeze.

In the interval he had apparently decided against visiting the Cathedral at all that morning and proposed instead to call on the Bishop. It was *costumbre* for visitors to the town to be taken to the Bishop if—and here he stiffly bowed—they were deserving of the honour. On the way to the Palace he pointed out the landmarks of the town, every one relating to days gone by: the houses of former notables, their descendants now ruined or dead or moved to the capital, the one-time *casa consistorial* and the little *plaza*, named after Alfonso XIII, in front of the Cathedral itself where once they held their bull-fights. They used to form an arena by barricading the narrow lanes that ran down into it, while the people looked on from the surrounding windows: an ideal place and an ideal arrangement, he said, but one which resulted in countless deaths. Shakily mounting the Palace stairs, he sang the praises of the Bishop: a Castilian, true, but for once a good Castilian. The door was opened by a smooth, pale and governessy chaplain, who kept us waiting for a decent interval before showing us with an important flurry of skirts into the Bishop's reception room. This was large and airy, simply but beautifully furnished with eighteenth-century tables and chairs, the coverings and hangings being all of a rich yellow silk, and it had a little the air of a lady's parlour at Versailles. Here sat the Bishop himself, brown and chubby, smiling a fatherly welcome.

I had not expected to hobnob with bishops this morning: I was dressed for different occasions altogether, being bare-legged and in a garment with short sleeves, a garment, furthermore, that had been so attenuated by Spanish dry-cleaning that, as I knelt to kiss the episcopal ring, there was a moment's hideous doubt of my being able to rise again. To add to the embarrassment of these circumstances, Don Eduardo now introduced me with the magniloquence of his race as "a famous author": at the same time laying a clawlike hand on his breast in a manner to show that any glory knocking about developed also on him. But there was a good Castilian twinkle in the Bishop's eye, and he appeared to be familiar with Don Eduardo's modes of expression. Folding his hands across his comfortable belly, he began amiably and in a refreshingly pure accent to discourse on subjects he presumed of interest: Galicia, Celts, the coloration of Celtic hair and the shape of Celtic skulls, the Bretons, the Welsh, the Irish, the Gallegan fishermen that sail in Ireland's waters every year (to the great annoyance of the local inhabitants, had he but known it), of strange portents and marvels and especially of a miracle that once befell a Gallegan Bishop—with the help of God, of course, and here he sketched the sign of the cross in the air—and then, having politely inquired after my book and made a few suggestions, he indicated, *suaviter in modo*, that the interview was at an end.

"You must write the truth about all of us here," he said with a brighter twinkle than ever, "but please write it *con cariño*."

Don Eduardo complacently fondled his beard and, once outside the door, declared that the Bishop was well pleased with the visit. He had a beautifully proprietary attitude toward such matters. But to me these encounters with the Hierarchy ever appear as tending towards the unilateral.

At six o'clock of that afternoon the beard came jauntily waving up the street to the Hospedaje Galicia, all set for a tour of the Cathedral. By now Don Eduardo and I were popularly assumed to be courting, and smiling faces greeted us the length of the way. He looked as frail as a dead leaf, all skin and bone and beard, but when it came to revealing and expounding the glories of Mondoñedo he had the endurance of a lion. Indeed, there were only two interests in his life, the people said, and none could tell which came first, the town or his beard. This he would ever proudly caress as he hobbled along, and he would not have cut it for ten thousand pesetas. He was also the natural and implacable enemy of all innovation and viewed with a jaundiced eye the rising tide of progress in Mondoñedo, such as cemented paving in place of the cobbles and stones and new street-lighting instead of the old iron *faroles*. He told me now that in the "good days" Mondoñedo had been the capital of the province, but, this honour having unwisely been passed to Lugo in the last century, today merely existed in "the shadow of the Cathedral." There was no life in the place but the Cathedral's life.

A Canon of the chapter was waiting at the main door to accompany us round it. He was a fat and charming man with a great simplicity of manner and he appeared to be highly amused by Don Eduardo, who continually broke into his account of things and filled it out with copious, rambling informations of his own. It was delightful to see the pride they both took in the most ordinary objects. Don Eduardo's conversation abounded in phrases such as "simple, yes, but attractive" and "not elegant, truly, but well made," uttered with a look of appeal at the Canon and me in turn. Then the Canon would begin: "Here are some more paintings," and he would at once burst in with: "They cannot really be called remarkable!" "Yet not to be despised!" would be the Canon's warm rejoinder, and he would quickly agree: "No, no! Never to be despised!" There was in fact a lovely rose window, several interesting murals of the twelfth century and illustrations to the Litany of the Blessed Virgin in charming colour above the high altar, a massive baroque reredos in gold and La Inglesa herself, who alone in the Cathedral had the honour of the Santisimo reserved in her chapel. She was, candidly, a frump, with her long, florid face, heavy-cheeked and short-nosed, and her Saxon tresses; and matters had not been improved by a clumsy, Spanish crown of the eighteenth century being clapped on her head, where it leaned tipsily to one side. But she is greatly loved and venerated by the local people, and every year many of the faithful visit her from all parts of the region: foreigners, whether of flesh or wood, usually get off to a flying start in Spain.

The Canon said that the history of Mondoñedo was but the history of her successive Bishops. One Bishop built the sacristy, another put in the rose window, another donated the beautiful drinking-fountain away down the road to the people's use: everywhere, in everything, was "*la mano del Obispo.*" He led the way to the chapter house, whose walls were lined with portraits of these holy men, their facial expression for the most part anything but spiritual. I asked if Napoleon had passed by here, and Don Eduardo's slender frame quivered and his great hollow eyes burned with passion as he described the horrible deeds of the French troops, as well as the patriotism of the chapter in giving their rents for the defense of the country and the heroism of the militias. An English general had been quartered in the very room where now we stood, and the Bishop of the time had written an ode to him: falling into a dramatic posture, he made as if to recite it, but the words did not come and he fretfully remarked that he must be growing old.

At the end of the tour I made a suitable offering to the Cathedral, at which the Canon seized my hand and gently waved it up and down, declaring that God Himself would pay it back, and with interest added, while Don Eduardo stood by and grunted his approval. And all the way to the seminary, our next appointment, he boasted of the incomes the prelates of former times enjoyed: forty million pesetas! The people respected their Bishops once! How different from today! It didn't do to think about it much! And he dolefully wagged his head as if the decline in proper feeling were indeed too fearful to contemplate.

We now made the acquaintance of the Rector, head of a seminary which trained three hundred boys at a time, from the ages of ten to twenty-four. He was as sweet a character as the Canon himself, and as much entertained by Don Eduardo, whose panegyrics on his learning, goodness and wisdom overleaped all bounds of discretion or probability. The Rector had the same innocent pride in modest possessions as the others, and he drew particular attention to the tasteless modern chapel and to a real ostrich egg from Africa in the natural history department. He seemed to be less impressed by the library, which was very impressive indeed. Hundred upon hundred of wonderful old books and maps, some of them unique, were all higgledy-piggledy together, many with worms burrowing into their ancient leaves—"Worm powder costs such a lot," the Rector observed with a sigh, carefully shutting a volume so as not to alarm the occupants—others with torn bindings, some again duplicated, so that with a little trouble they could have been exchanged for ones that were lacking, and everywhere dust, disorder and confusion, a veritable bibliophile's nightmare. Lightheartedly the Rector crumpled the pages in turning them over or, licking his thumb to get a better purchase, left a huge black smear across them: what sort of handling they got from the little seminarists, one hardly cared to imagine.

When we had seen the last classroom and the last dormitory, we returned to Don Eduardo's own little house. Here was delightful confusion again, floor, chair and table being piled high with dusty notes in a spiky handwriting: bundle upon bundle, seemingly unpaged, all related to the history of Mondoñedo and all, he declared, to be published in the fullness of time. There were also a number of rusty swords on the wall, and everywhere else a crowd of holy images, crucifixes, mementoes and bits of old china, French and English. On the top of a cupboard rode a dusty old chamber-pot. The portrait of his father showed a distinguished-looking old gentleman with a beard if anything longer than his own; and there was one of Rabindranath Tagore cut from a Madrid periodical, equally, it may be fancied, for the sake of his flourishing silver beard, as there seemed no other point of spiritual affinity. A picture of Don Eduardo himself had a little posy of dried flowers stuck piously in the frame. With enormous satisfaction he showed me the chronicles of the Santar family from their early days to the present time, in a thick album bound in vellum and with long, long Spanish pedigrees at the beginning. It was indeed the dwelling of a dedicated man. He told me that he lived entirely alone, except that a woman came in every day to clean the house and prepare his food. I would have given much for a few words with this lady, but she later proved to be a figment of his leaping imagination, a phantom retainer such as might have been recruited by Don Quixote himself: the people told me the house was never cleaned and that Don Eduardo had no cooked meals.

He took his leave with a last magnificent, cascading torrent of Spanish civilities and pressed into my arms a bundle of copies of a local newspaper, which appeared sporadically as occasion demanded and which turned out to be written entirely by himself. Column after column bore his signature at the head and a crowd of notes at the foot, most of them referring the reader to works written by him, although in nearly every case, as he frankly explained in brackets, these had yet to be published.

He must have been one of the finest and purest enthusiasts in the country. The only other I knew to come anywhere near him was a certain hairdresser in Madrid. He was not a leading or a fashionable hairdresser: he took three and a half hours to finish a customer and the results were then not wholly satisfactory, as he not only framed the face in a bower of repulsive kiss-curls, but sprayed them with fixative, making it impossible to brush them out. But he could recite endlessly from the Spanish classics. "I love all literature, good and bad," he would cry; and, as he pushed one's head under the boiling soapy water, there might burst from his lips the impassioned soliloquy of Don Juan in the cemetery:

> ¿Y no pasa veces mil
> que, en febril exaltación,
> ve nuestra imaginación
> como ser y realidad
> la vacia vanidad
> de una anhelada ilusión? . . .

"I should have been a poet myself," he would say ruefully, pouring a little more water down one's neck.

Very early next morning there was a commotion beneath the windows of the Hospedaje, as if a popular rising were under way; but it was only the young of Mondoñedo setting forth to Ribadeo, a place on the coast a few hours' journey away, where the people were to have their *gran fiesta*. A tiny, antique bus stood patiently in the midst of the seething throng, and it seemed at first as if all the shouting would only be over the question of who was to ride in it. This proved to be wrong, however, as all of them intended to. Before my astonished eyes the company squeezed itself in, man by man, and when at last the interior was full to bursting, with displaced heads and arms protruding from every window, the remainder climbed on the roof, or clung to the door, or lay spreadeagled on the hood. The uproar had been no more than a friendly morning conversation; and the hellish discomfort they were about to endure was for the sake of some coloured lights, the loudspeakers bellowing jazz and a few rockets. In the dawn of tomorrow they would all pile into the bus again, to be home in time for work. How much the outing meant to them could be judged from the distress of the skeleton staff left behind at the Hospedaje, a small girl of fifteen who continually sniffed and dabbed at her eyes with a handkerchief, and was not by any means to be consoled. And what difference they made to the town was felt the moment the little bus disappeared, coughing and swaying, away down the dusty road. Sleepy enough before, Mondoñedo now became a shell, a hospice for the dying: the men and women were labouring out on the hillside, and only the bent figures of the old crept about its dishevelled lanes, only the jangling bells of the Cathedral broke now and again on its senile repose.

But now August was half gone and in the first days of September I was to sail from Vigo for England. There remained a list of things, a *cruzero* of particular merit here, carved figures of the Celtic age there and an outlying *cronista* or two, that local patriots had assured me must be seen at whatever cost. But in three months I had covered over fifteen hundred miles in forced marches, and Spanish buses and Spanish inns now figured luridly in my dreams: such mind as I possessed had become like a full sponge, taking nothing in: and the better plan seemed to go to Pontevedra and laze away the last days there or on one of the exquisite little beaches of the neighbourhood.

In the old capital, now gaily beflagged and illumined for her *gran fiesta*, there was an animation and a *muchedumbre* such as it seldom knew, and they were setting up extra beds in the stately Parador as if it had been a casualty clearing station. Yet there were greybeards who said it was nothing like the spectacle of former times, instancing among much else the fact that the *corridas de delfines* had died out: although there can hardly have been one who had ever actually witnessed them. A vivid description of this singular entertainment is to be found in the memoirs of Don Prudencio Landin Tobio, a former *cronista* of the city. Days before they were needed, the dolphins were rounded up by the fishermen of La Moureia, using a special net of heavy hemp and copper wire for the purpose, and then corralled in the reaches between the Corbaceiras and the far shore of Poyo. In some years the creatures would fail to appear at all when required, and then the *corrida* would have to be cancelled, to the bitter grief of the public. The dolphins were fought by men in boats, who were armed with harpoons attached to a long cord, and with knives and cutlasses for close-quarter work; and, in their vain attempts to escape, the poor things would dive under these boats and often upset them, so that men and dolphins all struggled together in water encarmined by their blood, while the people on shore participated by throwing stones or even shooting. Sometimes in despair the animals tried to rush the net in a body, but boats full of armed men waited here too to head them back. When the last of them had been slaughtered, their bodies were cut up and the oil extracted, to pay for repairs to the net, which would be left in a shocking condition. The sport was greatly appreciated in Portugal as well, in the province of Algarbe, but has disappeared there too.

The greybeards had to be content with bulls, of which there were to be three engagements, with the stars—Aparicio, Ortega and Jumillano—on the first day, the aspiring novices on the second, and a comic taurine spectacle on the third. On the eve of the first *corrida* the bulls were receiving visitors in their pen to one side of the ring. Until then I had only seen them rage about in the arena, and expected them to stamp and snort, whisk their tails and try their horns and glare about with an eye like a crimson lollipop; but they were very gentle and quiet, with disturbingly babyish faces, and some of them lay resting in a shadowy corner. Their keeper said they were always calm and good, and never offered harm to anyone who came feeding or helping them; but their blood got up at once when they entered the ring and heard the people roar.

The ring at Pontevedra was small, a private property, and packed to overflowing on the first day. Unless every mother's son present had come over from Portugal, I felt more dubious than ever about Don Felipe's contention that Gallegos do not care for the fight: particularly when I caught sight of Don Felipe himself in the crowd. And, *caramba!* there was the *dueña* of the kip on the Vigo waterfront, her pouter's bosom higher than ever, terrifyingly smart in flowered silk and much given to poking her escort in the ribs with a fan. And the *dueño* of the España in Santiago, a trim, melancholy young man who took little interest in his hotel, but lay reading in bed for most of the day. And the Cuban Consul, wearing a jaunty yachting cap and greeting his hosts of friends with flashes of gold teeth in every direction. There too was the usual bewildering number of immensely stout ladies, between a pair of whom as ever I was tightly wedged; and the usual fat man who sank down in relief on his paper cushion which exploded with a loud report, to the great joy of *aficionados* around, who can never see this simple occurrence too often. As usual, too, the bulk of the audience arrived at the very moment when the *corrida* was due to begin, and great numbers of people then were found to be sitting in the wrong places, causing indescribable confusion and vexing the fighters, who, dressed in all their glittering splendour, were peering crossly round the arena gates.

The best turn of the afternoon was a brilliantly comic passage during the interval, when a water-cock plumb in the middle of the sand could by no means be stopped flowing and the rising tide threatened to transform the arena into a marsh. Even the stars forgot their dignity and ran up to stare and laugh, even as on great religious and national parades a Spanish guard of honour will often spontaneously fall out in order to get a better view of the proceedings. Otherwise it was remarkable only for the fury of the people at Ortega with his second bull. It was clearly not his day. The first had embedded his right horn in a wooden post like an axe within a few seconds of appearing, and Ortega had no stomach for the other: his *faena* was of the briefest, and he gave the horns the widest possible berth; and the *suerte* was so horribly bungled that a storm of whistles and boos went up, accompanied by a rain of missiles. And for once the crowd was quite implacable. Aparicio followed splendidly, but they paid little attention to him, being far too busy chanting in chorus, *"Fuera, Ortega! Fuera, Ortega!"* (Hop it, Ortega!) whenever the unhappy fellow showed his nose in the ring; and that night in a number of Pontevedran windows his photograph appeared, raised to lasting shame by the caption *Ortega el Carota* (Fat-face Ortega). He is a celebrated fighter of long experience, and as brave and skilful as the next: it was no more than one of the infernal misfortunes of a *torero's* life.

Next day, by contrast, the three young boys covered themselves with glory and were carried shoulder-high through the town to their hotel. I never saw it, having left after the second bull. *Novilladas* are for people who love to shudder and are not dismayed by the prospect of terrible events. The fighters are little more than children, wonderfully brave and determined to do or die: they make one mistake after another, saving themselves time and again by the quickness of their young limbs and by their as yet unbroken nerve. To make matters worse, they cannot afford to pay a good team to support them, and must often depend on a motley crew of middle-aged throw-outs, chiefly concerned with preserving their own skins.

There was, this afternoon, something enormously pathetic about the three tense young faces as the company stood before the President's box to salute him. The first child was a handsome prodigy, and the crowd was with him from the beginning —for these occasions it keeps all the generosity so lacking towards established men—but when the sword had done its work, dropping the bull clean in his tracks like a rifle-shot, he ran to the side and leaned against it like a fainting girl. The ovation and the award of two ears restored him magically, however; and it was charming to see him refuse to throw those ears up to the crowd, as etiquette demanded, but stoutly hold on to them for himself, or perhaps his mother. The second child was twice knocked down, gored in the thigh and carried round for fifteen yards or so most ignominiously disposed between the bull's horns, and unable to bear it I went away, missing a brilliant kill and all the other feats of a notable afternoon. But later on in the evening, passing a hotel, I did have a glimpse of a fantastically ancient Rolls-Royce, with shabby boxes of capes piled on the roof and standing beside it the three happy little fellows, with flushed cheeks and eyes that shone with pride.

The festivities had been planned with laudable care and a program, beautifully designed and printed on excellent paper, explained what would take place and where at each hour of the day. Yet it bore little or no relation to the event. Arriving at twelve o'clock for the concert under the trees in the Alameda, we would find the bandstand empty and the instruments leaning drunkenly against the chairs. Instead of a *pasodoble*, a netball match would be in progress, played fiercely and intently on the high road beside the gardens, with the police scaring the traffic away and the crowd screaming instructions to and threats against the referee, while from the be-aproned balconies of the Diputación Provincial bald-headed senior officials looked down in approval. Or a fabulous organ recital of devotional classics by a distinguished Franciscan would be scheduled for the Sunday morning in the Church of San Francisco: whereas all that happened there was that a large plain girl was married to a trembling little man, who seemed greatly puzzled by the quantity of strangers assisting at his Nuptial Mass. As luck would have it, I was not to be defrauded of this particular treat, for, having dropped into the dusty shadows of Santa Maria for a moment's peace and quiet, I came on the recital in full swing. A school of orphan boys, their shaven heads scarred by ringworm, were gabbling the Rosary at the tops of their voices, led by nuns who appeared to be under the impression that this was a new form of Office; and on a wheezy organ, in which certain notes were missing fire like the notes of an ancient hurdy-gurdy, the good friar was working away at a familiar, secular song of Schubert's, under the impression, no doubt, that it was the *Ave Maria*.

In the evening, however, exactly as promised, Our Lady the Divine Pilgrim sallied forth on her chariot, to the accompaniment of rockets, furious church bells and a military band, escorted by a Cardinal and a Bishop, by minor clergy and acolytes, Maids of Honour in blue satin and gold crowns perched on the chariot itself like the mascots on a cake, goose-stepping soldiers, friars with lighted candles, all shuffling along at a snail's pace round the town while the crowds grew ever denser and more unmanageable, until one distracted Guardia municipal went so far as to let his revolver off in the air: an act thought by the multitude to be entirely in keeping with local sentiment and received with mighty applause. And when at last the Pilgrim was safely home again, they streamed joyously off to the fair in the gardens, where, under the rows and rows of coloured lights, they danced to the loudspeakers bawling out seven or eight different tunes at a time, or competed for weird, inappropriate prizes by kicking or shooting or guessing, or drank the Bilbao beer guaranteed as "the densest in Spain and of a classic flavour," or lined up patiently for the show of freaks, outside which a miserable panting sheep, chained on a pedestal the whole clock round, feebly waved its fifth leg.

For three days and nights the tumult continued, mounting steadily in pitch; and on the fourth we awoke to find the visitors suddenly gone and Pontevedra her drowsy self once more. The heartfelt self-congratulation of the local paper was all that kept the memory of the frolic alive. Money had been poured out, the money that always, mysteriously, is forthcoming in Spain to dazzle the outer world with a show and can never be found for bread and boots. The people had displayed the electric vitality, the impassioned endurance that none would suspect who only saw them engaged in their daily tasks. Now the dust began to settle on the aged yellow walls again and workmen dozed on benches or in the shade of trees.

It was agreeable to saunter through empty streets and to find a place in my favourite café. It was delightful too, to be met there with a welcoming smile instead of a harassed shrug of the shoulders. But it was something of a shock to hear the waiter exclaim with a wink as he poured the beer—in the good Spanish way, with six inches of foam to one of liquid—"*¡Aha! no le gustan a Usted los toros!*" There is something horrifying about the Spanish grapevine. I had slunk out of that bull-ring as unobtrusively as could be, and here was a strange man at the other end of the town fully informed of the matter. Whatever else may not work in Spain there is no fault to be found with the intelligence service; and this came home to me yet more vividly when at last I took my leave of Don Vicente in Vigo.

"And how was the festival? How were the bulls?" he asked. "Someone told me a foreign lady went out on the second day."

"It was I."

"They told me that too," he said gravely and sadly, "but I didn't believe it."

Oh misplaced loyalty! Ah the pain of not being quite up to the country of one's predilection!

The last few golden days slipped by. Something happens to time in Spain: all goes slowly but the hours. Now there waited in Vigo port the luxury cruiser on which Don Vicente with his wonted ingenuity had secured me a berth. How a vacancy could ever have occurred in this floating Paradise I cannot imagine, unless there had been a suicide. It left one evening at sundown, a brass band gaily playing "D'ye ken John Peel," the emerald of the Vigo hills, the rose-madder tints on the water's calm surface, reflected in the paper hats that were breaking out like a rash all over the saloon.

"Pity you couldn't have done the whole cruise."

Yes.

"By the way, what's your Christian name?"

Honor.

"Well, Honor . . ."

There is no place like home, anywhere.

HONOR TRACY started writing after the war, when she was living in Dublin. In Ireland she was associated with an Irish literary review edited by Sean O'Faolain. She also wrote short stories and articles for English and American periodicals.

Miss Tracy has had three earlier books published in England —two non-fiction books on Japan and Ireland, and a short novel, *The Deserters*.

She wrote THE STRAIGHT AND NARROW PATH, a modern classic, in Italy in the fall of 1954, while recovering from a long illness. SILK HATS AND NO BREAKFAST is her account of her travels in Spain, where she spent the summer of 1955.

Date Due

MAR 14 1970			
SE 13 '80			
	GB	PRINTED IN U. S. A.	